Phillips Academy
Andover

THE CAMPUS GUIDE

Phillips Academy
Andover

An Architectural Tour by
Susan J. Montgomery and Roger G. Reed
Photographs by Walter Smalling Jr.

Princeton Architectural Press
NEW YORK | 2000

This book has been made possible through the generous support
of the Graham Foundation for Advanced Studies in the Fine Arts.

Princeton Architectural Press
37 East 7th Street
New York, NY 10003
212.995.9620

For a free catalog of other books published by Princeton Architectural Press,
call toll free 1.800.722.6657 or visit www.papress.com

Editing: Jan Cigliano
Design: Sara E. Stemen
Maps: Jane Garvie
Special thanks to Ann Alter, Eugenia Bell, Caroline Green, Beth Harrison,
Mia Ihara, Clare Jacobson, Leslie Ann Kent, Mark Lamster, Anne Nitschke,
Lottchen Shivers, Jennifer Thompson, and Deb Wood of Princeton Architectural Press
—Kevin C. Lippert, *publisher*

Library of Congress Cataloging-in-Publication Data

Montgomery, Susan J., 1947–
  Phillips Academy / Susan J. Montgomery and Roger G. Reed ; color photographs by
  Walter Smalling, Jr.
    p. cm.—(The campus guide)
    Includes index.
    1. Phillips Academy—Buildings—Guidebooks. 2. Phillips
  Academy—Buildings—Pictorial works. I. Reed, Roger G., 1950- II. Smalling, Walter.
III
    Title. IV. Campus guide (New York, N.Y.)

LD7501.A5 M65 2000   CIP
727'2097445—dc21   00-020790

Printed in Hong Kong
04 03 02 01 00   5 4 3 2 1   First Edition

Students and faculty on the steps of Stone Chapel

*Dedicated to the students of Academy Hill,
past, present and future*

Abbot girls, 1890s

Seminarians at Stowe House

*Phillips Academy
commencement, 1894*

How to use this book

This guide is intended for visitors, alumni, and students who wish to have an insider's look at the most historic and interesting buildings on Phillips Academy's campus from Samuel Phillips Hall and Cochran Chapel to the Addison Gallery of American Art, the Peabody Museum of Archaeology, Abbot Academy, and Moncrieff Cochran Sanctuary.

The book is divided into five Walks. Each Walk covers a specific area of the campus and opens with a three-dimensional aerial map that locates the buildings on the walk. Following an introductory essay of the area, the major buildings on the Walk are illustrated with color photographs, and historical and architectural profiles.

Phillips Academy is a private boarding school of high-school age students, a community of resident faculty and their families, and staff members. Many of the buildings on campus are homes to these individuals—day and night. Please respect their privacy and safety. Please do not enter classrooms or residential buildings.

Phillips Academy buildings are closed to the public, except for the following:
Addison Gallery of American Art open: 10AM to 5PM Tuesday–Saturday,
    1PM to 5PM Sunday, closed Monday; closed August.
    978.749.4015.
Phillips Academy Archive, Oliver Wendell Holmes Library open: by
    appointment. 978.749.4069.
Cochran Chapel open: daily when school is in session.
George Washington Hall open: daily when school is in session.
Robert S. Peabody Museum of Archaeology open: 12PM to 5PM
    Tuesday–Saturday, closed Sunday–Monday, closed August.
    978.749.4490.
Phillips Hall, Office of Public Safety: 978.749.4444.
Andover Inn: 978.475.5903.

Further information:
    Phillips Academy
    Office of Public Information
    Andover, Massachusetts 01810
    978.749.4675
    www.andover.edu

The Vista

The Campus Guide: Phillips Academy, Andover could not have been written without the generous cooperation of many individuals. The authors of essays in our companion volume, *Academy Hill: The Andover Campus, 1778 to the Present,* contributed countless hours to the careful reconstruction of our campus' history. They have all enriched our understanding of the spirit of the schools on Academy Hill and the devotion of their founders, visionaries, donors, architects, and planners. Paul Turner's considerable knowledge of American college campuses provided us with a yardstick with which to measure the unique quality of Academy Hill. David Chase's meticulous and tenacious research unearthed names, dates, and circumstances surrounding the earliest buildings on campus, details that had been lost until now. Roger G. Reed, co-author of this guide, applied his expertise to the Victorian era buildings, giving us new appreciation for a rich part of our heritage that has largely vanished. Cynthia Zaitzevsky's scholarship encouraged us to look more carefully at the remarkable work of the renowned Olmsted firm, and Kimberly Alexander Shilland brought us into the twentieth century, raising our awareness that more than a generation has passed since the extraordinary growth of the 1960s occurred. It is now part of an impressive history. Finally, Susan C. Faxon, curator and assistant director of the Addison Gallery of American Art,

Andover Chapel detail

has provided not only an essay on the early twentieth-century history of the campus, but the guiding vision for this book and *Academy Hill* as well. Her dedication to this project, her sympathetic editing, and her willingness to share her detailed knowledge about this campus are much appreciated.

The staff of Phillips Academy has responded cheerfully to every request and query. Ruth Quattlebaum, Archivist of Phillips Academy, has patiently plowed through files, searched out photographs, and dispensed endless bits of advice and encouragement. The Office of Physical Plant has given us access to their files, architectural plans, and even remote sections of buildings.

We would especially like to thank Neil McEleney and Jack P. Skotz. Thomas J. Conlon, Director of Public Safety, and his department have offered their support and advice on numerous occasions. Michael E. Williams, Director of Facilities, has generously shared the resources of his department, including photographs and the Historic Buildings Report commissioned by his department in 1994.

Elm Arch

The staff of the Addison Gallery of American Art, as always, has pulled together to make this guide a reality. Juliann D. McDonough has expedited photograph requests and assisted with proofreading. Director Adam D. Weinberg had supported this project wholeheartedly. Boston University graduate intern Ellen Roberts has shared her enthusiasm, careful eye, and attention to detail to every phase of the manuscript. Frank Graham patiently copied archival photographs, often on short notice.

The staff of Princeton Architectural Press has guided us through a very tight publication schedule with patience and professionalism. We are honored to be the first secondary school included in their prestigious college campus guide series. In particular, we would like to thank our editor, Jan Cigliano, and former art director Sara Stemen for their fine work. Walter Smalling Jr.'s beautiful photography and personal good humor have made an ambitious project less stressful. Jane Garvie's elegant maps bring visual clarity to complex directions.

Barbara Thibault, Director of the Andover Historical Society, has generously shared her prodigious knowledge of the history of local buildings and people, as well as the resources of the society's archive. Finally, I would like to offer a personal note of gratitude to my co-author, Roger G. Reed. His extensive and exemplary *Phillips Academy Historical Buildings and Landscapes Survey* of 1994 provided the essential basis of research for these walking tours, and his thoughtful comments have fine-tuned our narrative.

Susan J. Montgomery
Research Associate
Addison Gallery of American Art

Foreword

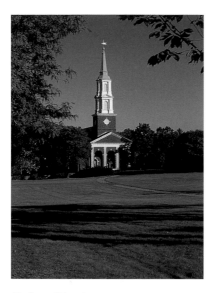

Cochran Chapel

Beautiful places, places where we have had formative experiences, always stay with us. The campus of Phillips Academy is such a place, working its powerful magic on generations of Andover students. They come back years later to find a favorite spot on campus—the Armillary Sphere, the lawn beneath a majestic elm, one of the pews in Cochran Chapel, the steps of Samuel Phillips Hall, a classroom in Pearson. Everywhere they turn, memories rush back.

Why is this place so powerful? Why does it play such an important role in the education of Andover students? There is something about being a part of this campus that calls forth the best and the finest in all of us. As students and teachers walk from place to place on the campus, they take their measure against a spacious and graceful landscape. They sense how they might fit into a greater scheme, how they can strive to do their very best work, how to uphold the high ideals that the history and mission of the academy have always meant to students and faculty.

How can mere brick and wood and granite, trees and expanse of lawn carry so much weight? No one can say exactly. But understanding how generations of academy leaders, trustees, donors, architects, and builders brought this present campus into being helps us to understand its present power and sets the very highest standard for those who plan for the future of the campus.

Barbara Landis Chase
Head of School
Phillips Academy

Introduction to the Phillips Academy Campus

Samuel Phillips Hall

As one approaches Phillips Academy, it is easy to believe that this picture-perfect campus has quietly existed in the classic New England community of Andover since 1778. But educational communities are abstract concepts, conceived by founders and perpetuated in the hearts and minds of students, faculty, and alumni. The campus, especially an old one, is a physical manifestation of that spirit. It adapts to changing educational theory, social and religious mores, and personal leadership, albeit hampered by the vicissitudes of finances and fate. In this, Andover is no different than any other preparatory school. What is unusual, however, is the fact that the campus has remained on the hill where the academy was established more than 220 years ago. It has been fortunate to have enough land available to expand when necessary and wise enough to recognize the value of its heritage. The campus is now recognized as the Academy Hill National Historic District and is listed on the National Register of Historic Places.

The campus as it is today actually encompasses four individual institutions founded over a span of fifty years: Phillips Academy (1778), Andover Theological Seminary (1808), the Teachers' Seminary (1827), and Abbot Academy (1828). Each school contributed buildings and affected changes in the campus as its fortune rose or fell. Today the seminaries are gone and Abbot has combined with Phillips, yet the academy's educational direction and physical resources have been enriched by their presence.

Architectural historian Paul Venable Turner has aptly applied the concept of *palimpsest*, a manuscript that has been written, erased, and re-written, to the Andover campus. Turner maintains that, "At Andover the palimpsest is multiple and irregular, with successive writings, partial erasures, transpositions, and revisions."[1] Academic buildings here were built, remodeled, demolished, destroyed by fire, and relocated with a fair degree of regularity, and the evidence of this 200-year-long process can still be read. This Campus Guide leads visitors geographically through most of the campus' 500 acres, while providing historical background to foster appreciation of not just the buildings and landscape features that remain, but the palimpsest of those that existed in the past.[2]

Samuel Phillips Jr.

Phillips Academy was founded in 1778 by Samuel Phillips Jr. (1752–1802), Harvard graduate, state legislator, and a prominent local businessman. Alarmed by the social turmoil of the Revolution, Phillips recognized that one way to restore solid values in America would be to establish a school for boys. "Youth is the important period," he wrote, "on the improvement or neglect of which depend the most important consequences to individuals and the community." Thus, the constitution of Phillips Academy states that in addition to formal education, the school would strive to teach "the Great End and Real Business of Living." With the financial backing of his father, Squire Samuel Phillips, who lived in Andover's North Parish (now North Andover), and his uncle, Dr. John Phillips of Exeter, New Hampshire, Phillips Academy opened its doors to thirteen students in April 1778.

From 1778 to 1865 Phillips Academy operated with no discernible "campus." From the beginning, it occupied individual, unrelated buildings. After the Andover Theological Seminary was founded in 1808, the academy seemed to exist only on the fringes of its more conspicuous offspring. The first classes were held in a former carpenter's shop at the corner of Main and Phillips Street, a temporary arrangement at best. In 1785, the so-called "second Academy," a large, two-story, wooden schoolhouse with student recitation rooms and a meeting hall, was erected on the other side of Main Street near Salem Street, at the highest point on Academy Hill. When the wooden Academy burned in 1818, the "Brick Academy," now known as Bulfinch Hall was built on another site off Salem Street.

Other than the classroom building, the academy had virtually no facilities. There were no dormitories. There was no common dining hall. Academy boys boarded in private homes all around the neighborhood. There was no chapel. Students attended

Bulfinch Hall

Andover's South Parish meeting house until 1818.

The Andover Theological Seminary, on the other hand, was founded in 1808 as an institution of higher learning, the equivalent of a graduate school, rather than a boys' academy. Eliphalet Pearson, former preceptor of Phillips Academy, resigned his positions as professor and acting president at Harvard

Andover Theological Seminary before 1870

College, and returned to Andover to fulfill the dream he had shared with his friend Samuel Phillips, of establishing a seminary within the supportive embrace of the academy. Since Phillips' death in 1802, Pearson had been president of the board of trustees. Phillips' widow, Phoebe Foxcroft Phillips, and their son John supported Pearson wholeheartedly, pledging a considerable fortune toward his success. One by one, three formal brick buildings, similar to those being erected at Harvard, Yale, Brown, and Princeton, appeared on a ridge above a marshy meadow, set well back from the main road.

The first, Foxcroft Hall[3] (1809), served as dormitory, classroom, and chapel until the young institution outgrew it. By 1817 the trustees decided to devote Foxcroft entirely to housing. They hired the renowned Boston architect Charles Bulfinch to design Pearson Hall for new classrooms and a chapel. By 1821, the seminary again needed more dormitory space, and Bartlet Hall was erected in line with Pearson and Foxcroft Halls. The overall plan for the seminary included landscaping of the meadow as an open common and planting of an allée of English Elms, still called Elm Arch to this day. A modest wooden dining hall was built behind Seminary Row by 1810. An infirmary and an exercise building were added on the north side of Chapel Avenue, and across Main Street, the first four homes in "Faculty Row" appeared between 1809 and 1829. In only twenty years, the theological seminary had created a true campus that satisfied the personal and educational needs of students and teachers. It dominated Academy Hill and Phillips Academy, and remained essentially the same for the next forty years.

In the meantime, the trustees of the academy received a windfall bequest from William Phillips, an uncle of Samuel Phillips Jr. and longtime board member. They applied those funds toward the establishment of the third school on the hill, the Teachers' Seminary. Intended to train boys as grammar school teachers rather than prepare them for college, the Teachers' Seminary focused on a practical curriculum of reading and composition, mathematics, science, and some modern languages. Similar to Boston's

Stone Academy, 1857

well-known English and Latin public high schools, it was an "English" school in contrast to the "classical" Phillips Academy. The Teachers' Seminary was housed in its own stone building at the corner of Main Street and Chapel Avenue, near the site of the present Cochran Chapel. The school had no financial resources and attempted, unsuccessfully, to survive on tuition fees alone. In 1842, it was absorbed by the academy as the English Department. Twenty-two years later, the building, then known as the Stone Academy, was totally destroyed by fire.

For almost 60 years, from 1808 to 1865, the seminary and the academy coexisted. As academy boys came together for classes from boarding houses all over South Parish, they passed by Seminary Row. They attended services at the seminary chapel with the "Theologues." They were acutely aware of the prestigious institution that overshadowed their own, decidedly secondary, status. When the Stone Academy burned in December 1864, the trustees immediately seized the opportunity to create for the first time a distinct Phillips Academy campus. They sited its replacement on the west side of Main Street, well north of Faculty Row.

The trustees commissioned Boston architect Charles A. Cummings to design the new main Academy near the corner of Main and School Streets. The site may have been chosen because of the modest wooden dormitories that had been erected nearby in the mid-1830s: six Latin Commons for academy students, and six English Commons for pupils of the Teachers' Seminary. The new Academy was a four-story Venetian Gothic building with an imposing central pavilion, housing a large recitation room, classrooms, and the chapel. With some dormitories and a new academic building, and a privately run dining facility nearby, a semblance of an acad-

Phillips Hall, Graves Hall, the Main Academy, English Commons, and Draper Cottage

Brechin Hall

emy campus had been created. Graves Hall, designed by Merrill & Cutler of Lowell, Massachusetts, for the science department, was the next addition, following in two stages in 1883 and 1891. A small office building for the academy administration, called Phillips Hall, was erected in 1885, east of Graves. Small cottage style dormitories were built in the early 1890s on Old Campus Road, which ran parallel to Main Street, behind Faculty Row. This cluster of buildings was Phillips Academy well into the twentieth century.

Meanwhile, the theological seminary prospered on the east side of Main Street. In 1865 the trustees hired Charles A. Cummings to design another building on the hill, on the site of the wooden Academy that had burned in 1818. Named Brechin Hall, after the Scottish home town of three prosperous patrons in Andover, it housed a growing library on the second floor, with a museum honoring the seminary's graduates in missions all over the world at ground level. Cummings' Venetian Gothic building was surprisingly adventurous in taste for 1865; Brechin Hall predated by a year the more famous masterpiece of this style, Ware & Van Brunt's Memorial Hall at Harvard. In 1875, the seminary required a larger chapel and turned again to Charles Cummings, and his partner Willard T. Sears, who were then engaged in the construction of Old South Church on Boston's Copley Square. The traditional Gothic revival church served as chapel and assembly hall for over 50 years.

Samaritan House, Stowe House, and Stone Chapel

In the last quarter of the nineteenth century, just as Phillips Academy began to move out of the long shadow cast by the seminary, seminary enrollment and finances began to decline. By 1900 empty dormitory space in Seminary Row was rented to the academy. In 1908 the theological seminary left Andover entirely, and all of its property on the east side of Main Street was acquired by the academy.

The academy trustees did not immediately seize upon the seminary's property for expansion. In 1891 they had commissioned a master plan from Frederick Law Olmsted and Co., which laid out a series of dormitories and classroom buildings in a winding park-like setting behind Faculty Row. By 1903 the plan had changed to a more formal scheme of quadrangles, and the Olmsted firm had shifted the center of the academy campus farther south toward the top of the hill at the request of the trustees. When the seminary left Andover, the trustees were firmly committed to architect Guy Lowell's plan for a major new complex on the west side of Main Street. Three large dormitories, Bishop, Adams, and Taylor Halls, were erected there by 1913.

After a hiatus of construction during World War I, the trustees were ready to recommit to Lowell's plan in 1919: a huge central building housing classrooms, an auditorium, a chapel, and administrative offices, surrounded by a quadrangle of dormitories, with a memorial tower at the center. Objections to the site began to arise from trustees and alumni, drastically altering the future of the Andover campus. After much debate, Charles A. Platt of New York City was hired as a consulting architect. Platt's judgment was swift and sure: the academy should embrace the theological seminary campus and transform it into something bigger and better.

Guy Lowell, Drawing of Proposed Campus on the West Side, 1919

Memorial Bell Tower, 1923

By 1923 the transformation had begun. Lowell's bell tower, a memorial to Phillips Academy alumni killed during the war, was erected on the old Training Field at the corner of Main and Salem Streets. His design for the huge main Academy was rethought, resulting in two buildings, Samuel Phillips

Hall (1924) and George Washington Hall (1926). To give Samuel Phillips Hall center stage, Platt relocated Pearson Hall, the central building of Seminary Row. Under Platt's guidance, the buildings considered unsuitable to the new vision, including Brechin Hall and Stone Chapel, were demolished or relocated. Ten new colonial revival buildings took their places as prominent features of the new campus: a chapel, an art museum, a library, a dining hall, administration and classroom buildings and a new dormitory.

The Vista

Not everyone was cavalier about losing the old familiar buildings on the way to a modern campus. Headmaster Alfred Stearns, among others, was reluctant to disturb the historic character of Chapel Avenue and destroy the old Stone Chapel; Stearns complained repeatedly to Platt and to Thomas Cochran, one of the academy's most generous donors. Cochran acknowledged Stearns' surrender to Platt's judgment in June 1930,

> I think you show a great deal of broadmindedness and tolerance in accommodating yourself to the new Chapel in so generous a fashion. I can understand the feeling of sentiment that you felt in your heart and soul with respect to the old structure. Naturally, it is one that I do not happen to share.

In less than fifteen years, Platt imposed a new order on the central campus, an order that still dominates the hill almost seventy years later.

Charles A. Platt, Plan for the Ideal Andover

Phillips Gate, 1928
decorated for the sesquicentennial celebration

At Andover's sesqui-centennial anniversary cele-bration in 1928, the trustees presented two models of the academy to parents, alumni, and major donors. One showed the campus as it existed at that moment. The other, the "ideal Andover," offered a glimpse of the future

Commons

as they hoped it would be. In 1932, when Platt completed the Cochran Chapel as his last building for the school, everything proposed on the ideal model had been carried out. Nonetheless, this was not the end of change at Andover; the school continued to improve and add to its facilities through the 1930s. The infirmary needed to be updated. Bulfinch Hall should be restored to its "original" condition. At least one more dormitory was required if the academy was to house all of its students on campus. Additional faculty housing was imperative to attract the best teachers. Despite the Great Depression, all of these goals were accomplished by 1937.

The architects in charge of this second phase of projects were Perry, Shaw, & Hepburn of Boston. They had achieved national recognition as John D. Rockefeller's architects for an impressive new restoration in Virginia. Colonial Williamsburg established Perry, Shaw, & Hepburn's reputation as the preeminent colonial revival architects of their time. They were the perfect choice for the Andover campus, where Guy Lowell and Charles Platt had already established colonial revival as the style of choice. Perry, Shaw, & Hepburn designed a sympathetic addition to Lowell's Isham Infirmary and completed the West Quadrangle dormitories with a simple Georgian revival brick design for Rockwell House.

From 1936 to 1937, the firm worked on Bulfinch Hall, which had undergone a series of alterations and a disastrous fire since it was built in 1818. The exterior of the building was restored as accurately as possible, based on nineteenth-century photographic evidence. The interior, however, was designed to satisfy the twentieth-century preference for small, intimate classes, specifically for the English Department. William Graves Perry responded in classic colonial revival style: "the new construction has been guided . . . by the assumption that had the present problem arisen in Bulfinch's time, he might have solved it in a similar manner provided the outside shell were standing as it is today."[4]

In 1937 Perry, Shaw, & Hepburn designed five faculty houses at the end of Hidden Field Road, each one a unique interpretation of colonial revival design. They reflect the experienced, confident design skills of a firm recognized as masters of this style. Perry, Shaw, & Hepburn's first project on campus, some nine years earlier, shows the same level of skill and sophistication in another architectural genre. Davison House, originally the clubhouse for one of Andover's secret societies, was built in 1928 before colonial revival became the firm's trademark. It has an elegantly simple Tudor-inspired design, heightened by the judicious use of high quality materials.

Following World War II, Phillips Academy entered a period of architectural activity second only to the Lowell-Platt era. By the mid-1950s it was clear that enrollment was rapidly increasing and new dormitories became a priority. Educational and social theories had evolved. Classrooms became more democratic, more collaborative. Relationships between teachers and students became less formal. The Architects Collaborative, the

The Architects Collaborative, Rendering for Rabbit Pond Dormitory

prestigious Cambridge firm whose very name reflected the post-war mood of optimism and cooperation, was retained to do a campus wide master plan. Led by partner Benjamin Thompson, TAC identified short and long-term needs for new construction as well as proposals for renovation. Key to this "Andover Program" was a group of dormitories clustered around Rabbit Pond. Designed to meet new ideas of academic community and informal interaction among faculty and students, each Rabbit Pond dorm incorporated a common living room and clusters of student rooms. Thompson maintained the small scale and predominant use of brick elsewhere on campus, but interpreted those elements in a thoroughly modern style in buildings tucked into the rolling topography adjacent to Rabbit Pond.

Thompson's success with the dorms led to additional commissions on campus. The Thomas M. Evans Science Building of 1959 was the product of the "flexible laboratory" school of science education. Biology, chemistry and physics each had their own wing, with movable partitions. Evans was designed to stand alone behind Samuel Phillips Hall, and has been described as a modern outdoor sculpture, independent of other campus architecture.

The Elson Art Center, on the other hand, was designed as a link between two Platt buildings, the Addison Gallery of American Art and George Washington Hall. The making of art was given new importance in Andover's post-war curriculum. Studios and classrooms were needed to replace cramped, makeshift spaces in the basement of the Addison. Thompson's solution encloses the central campus on the Chapel Street side, except for a low, wide entry into a new courtyard. The courtyard façade has large plate glass windows onto studios and hallway galleries, revealing the activity inside to passers-by. At night, the building's structure disappears in the darkness and the light-filled interior space takes on the positive role of connecting link.

In 1973 Abbot Academy merged with Phillips and coeducation was introduced on Academy Hill. Founded in 1828, Abbot Female Academy was Andover's response to growing democratization in the young nation and

Abbot Hall, Smith Hall, and Davis Hall

a long-standing interest in the education of women.[5] It is said that Samuel Phillips Jr. had promised his wife Phoebe that they would establish a girls' school as soon as Phillips Academy, and presumably the theological seminary, were successfully launched. Although both Phillipses died before that happened, Mrs. Phillips held strong beliefs about female education and inspired her friend and confidante Samuel Farrar to take up her cause when the opportunity arose. That chance came in 1828 when a notice was circulated in Andover calling for those interested in a "Female High School" to come to a meeting. Among those who responded were Samuel Farrar, treasurer of the academy and seminary board of trustees since 1803, Mark Newman, former principal of Phillips Academy, and the ministers of local parishes. In May of 1829, the new academy opened in its own fashionable Greek revival building on School Street.

Abbot's curriculum was more progressive than its brother institution on the hill. In 1844 Abbot girls could study algebra and geometry, grammar, poetry, rhetoric, ancient and modern geography and history, a variety of sciences including biology, geology, physiology, and astronomy, philosophy and theology, as well as Latin, Greek, French, Italian and German, and drawing and painting. At mid-century it began to transform itself from a day school to a boarding school. In 1854 Smith Hall, a large Italianate dormitory was built by the Boston architect John Stevens and Harriet Beecher Stowe spearheaded a fundraising bazaar held by the ladies of Academy Hill, which raised $2,000 to furnish the interior.[6]

Five years later Phebe and Philena McKeen, sisters and educators from Vermont, arrived in Andover. Philena became principal; Phebe was her

Draper Hall

assistant and a teacher. Under Philena McKeen, an indefatigable fundraiser and lobbyist for her school, Abbot expanded to a twenty-two acre campus.

By the 1880s the physical plant was no longer adequate to the growing school and in typical fashion, Miss McKeen launched an ambitious campaign to alter the campus entirely. Hartwell & Richardson designed a master plan that called for the replacement of all existing buildings with an open quadrangle of Romanesque style buildings. Financial constraints forced a modification of the plan. The original Abbot Hall was moved 90 degrees to the north to make way for Draper Hall, a huge Richardsonian Romanesque dormitory. In 1904 McKeen Hall joined Draper on the south and in 1906, Andrews, Jaques, & Rantoul added the John-Esther Gallery to Abbot Hall. This completed the core of today's Abbot campus. In many ways the ability of Abbot Academy to provide adequate dormitory space, to modernize curriculum, and provide a coherent campus surpassed the efforts of the larger, wealthier, and more prestigious Phillips Academy just up the hill.

In the 1920s while Charles Platt was literally transforming the Phillips Academy campus, Abbot carried out a modest landscape plan designed by the Olmsted firm. Another dormitory was added in the late 1930s; an infirmary and a gymnasium followed. The academy was, in the 1950s, perhaps increasingly conservative in comparison to the "outside" world, but nevertheless it continued to grow in enrollment and reputation. It survived the competition of improved public education, and the post-war anti-elitist sentiment that made private schools seem somehow un-American. The 1960s were another mattter.

Abbot historian Susan McIntosh Lloyd defined the academy's last decade, 1963 to 1973 as nothing less than an assault:

> . . . the outside world beat upon Abbot's doors with such insistence that they must either be opened up or broken down. The Trustees opened them and the world rushed in like a clumsy repairman, knocking over tables and trampling valuable heirlooms, but also bringing fresh air into musty places, and piling on the floor a heap of lumber and tools with which to build anew.[7]

In 1973 Abbot Academy conceded to public clamor for reform of all kinds—social, philosophical, political, sexual, and educational. Despite radical change of administration toward, on the one hand, more professional management, and on the other a loosening of demanding regulations of behavior, coeducation seemed too powerful a force to resist.

Abbot officially merged with Phillips Academy in January 1973. Predictably, major obstacles to settling young women into a traditionally male school arose and were overcome. More difficult was the resolution for the Abbot campus, a cluster of buildings at least 70 years old, and for the most part no longer useful to the coed Phillips Academy. Buildings stood empty or ill-used and neglected until an effort began in the 1990s to recapture the Abbot spaces and adapt them to new uses. Abbot Hall and John-Esther Gallery now house offices, storage facilities, and a visiting artist apartment and studio. McKeen was renovated as offices and a community day care center. In 1996 Draper Hall was completely renovated as a combination of offices and faculty apartments. Although part of the building had to be demolished, its important front façade was saved and its critical role as the anchor of Abbot Circle was retained. Abbot campus is now largely a center of administrative activity.

Academy Hill today is the result of the merger of four campuses and 220 years of growth and change, the visual record, the palimpsest, of all who have made their mark here.

1.	Paul V. Turner, "The Campus as Palimpsest: Layers of History at Phillips Academy," in *Academy Hill: The Andover Campus, 1778 to the Present* (Andover, MA and New York: Addison Gallery of American Art and Princeton Architectural Press, 2000), 1.

2.	For a detailed history of the campus, see essays in *Academy Hill: The Andover Campus, 1778 to the Present*.

3.	The names of many buildings on the Andover campus have been changed over the years, some more than once. To avoid confusion, the *current* name has been used consistently, regardless of historical context. Where appropriate, the reason for the name change has been noted.

4.	William Graves Perry, "Bulfinch Hall Reconstructed," *The Andover Bulletin* 31 no. 5 (July 1937): 5–8.

5.	For a complete history of Abbot, see Susan McIntosh Lloyd, *A Singular School: Abbot Academy, 1828–1973* (Andover, MA: Phillips Academy, 1979).

6.	Lloyd, 75.

7.	Lloyd, 343.

The Campus Center

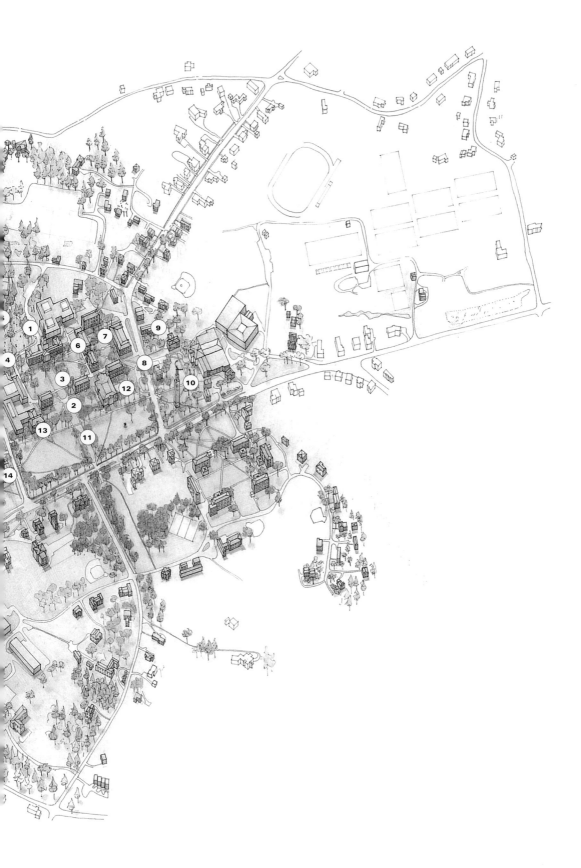

Academy Hill

At the heart of Phillips Academy is Samuel Phillips Hall, the largest class-room building at Andover. "Sam Phil," as it is affectionately called, presides over the Great Quadrangle from the top of the Vista, the dominant east-west axis of Academy Hill. As soon as its location was chosen in 1922, Sam Phil became the keystone for the central campus. It anchored the Vista's eastern end, allowing Charles Platt to expand the organizational plan on which the present campus developed.

Sam Phil also negotiated a dynamic balance between modern ambition and respect for the past. Twentieth-century planners, architects, donors, and administrators quite consciously created today's Phillips Academy campus on the foundation of the Andover Theological Seminary, a choice that is apparent from a vantage point inside the Great Quad. The early-nineteenth-century Seminary Row had survived intact for more than one hundred years, on what is now the west side of the Quad. When Phillips needed a new main classroom building in 1922, the school located it east of the row's three old buildings. Pearson Hall (1818), the center of the row, was moved aside to open the sight line to Sam Phil. Literally and symbolically, the old gave way for the new.

When it was completed, the new building was named Samuel Phillips Hall, after the founder of the academy. Over the next three years, the three old seminary buildings were integrated with new ones to create the Great Quad. Foxcroft (1809) and Bartlet (1821) remained where they were, a kind of honor guard for Sam Phil behind them. Pearson was relocated to the

Foxcroft, Pearson, and Bartlet Halls, 1907

Foxcroft, Samuel Phillips, and Bartlet Halls

south and paired with Morse Hall in 1927–1928. They faced another new building, George Washington Hall (1925–1926) on the north.

Nowhere is architectural historian Paul Turner's image of the Andover campus as palimpsest—a visible record of change over time—more clear than here on this central campus. The destinies of three of Academy Hill's four schools are entwined here. The oldest surviving academy building, Hardy House (1804–1805), is here. The three original seminary buildings are here. The newest structure is here as well, the Shuman Admission Center. The landscape and the buildings have been created, renovated, restored, even renamed, repeatedly, and yet the past is always present.

1. Samuel Phillips Hall *Guy Lowell, 1924*

Designed as the centerpiece of the new central campus, Samuel Phillips Hall is a clear expression of Guy Lowell's interpretation of colonial revival style. Not truly "colonial" or even eighteenth century in its sources, Sam Phil actually incorporates an exuberant mix of motifs popular in America in the 1840s. Grand in size and detail, the hall dominates the Great Quad.

A double flight of granite steps leads ceremoniously to the main entrance on a broad brick façade set on a high ashlar stone foundation. Two brick wings extend from the central block. At the center is a bold pedimented portico with six massive Doric columns, which supports a wooden bell tower with four clocks of luminous blue glass, an eclectic abundance of finials, and a copper-clad cupola. The tower, cupola, and weathervane rise to 117 feet, an imposing height even from the vantage point of Main Street.

Wooden window surrounds and cornice organize the red brick of the two wings. The double-hung windows have 20-over-20 lights on the first floor, 16-over-16 on the second. In 1923 a writer for *The Phillips Bulletin*

Samuel Phillips Hall

considered these small-paned sashes "suitable to the American Colonial architecture of the building. Those of the first storey," he went on, "are made especially interesting by a pillared balustrade below, and a pointed pediment over each one." (In fact, the outer windows have no pediments.)

The bold changes that led the school to create a 200-foot view to Sam Phil by removing Pearson Hall from Seminary Row in 1922 caused some alarm among alumni. However, when the new building opened in January 1924, *The Phillips Bulletin* reported, "Those alumni who have recently visited the Hill have been impressed by the stately dignity and charm of the new structure, which is in perfect harmony with the best of the older architecture around it."

The Vista

2. The Vista   *Charles A. Platt, 1928*

New York architect Charles Platt created the Vista to extend from the steps
of Sam Phil across the Great Quad, down the steps of the original seminary
terrace and across Main Street. As Phillips Academy's consulting architect,
Platt had recommended the site for Sam Phil in 1922, and had ordered the
relocation of Pearson Hall, Tucker House, and Bancroft Hall on the west side
of Main Street to accommodate the Vista. Clearly related to Platt's interest
in Italian landscape design, the Vista's formality imposed a new rigor on the
campus, transcending the interruption of a major thoroughfare and uniting
for the first time the eastern seminary campus with the academy's former
campus on the west.

The Vista also indicates the extent of control that Platt exercised
on the campus. Even before Samuel Phillips Hall was under construction,
Platt was maneuvering around Lowell as well as the Olmsted Brothers firm,
which had advised the trustees on landscape design and campus development for more than 25 years. Supported by the deep-pocketed Thomas
Cochran, who funded nearly all of the new buildings and landscaping of the
late 1920s and 1930s, Platt's scheme was virtually unopposed.

3. Seminary Row: *Foxcroft Hall, Pearson Hall, and Bartlet Hall*

Foxcroft Hall *1809*
Pearson Hall *Charles Bulfinch, 1817–1818*
Bartlet Hall *1821*

Although modified over the years, Foxcroft, Pearson, and Bartlet Halls are the three buildings erected between 1808 and 1821 for the newly founded Andover Theological Seminary. Fourteen years after the academy acquired the property in the early twentieth century, it began to create a new campus with Seminary Row at the center.

Foxcroft was originally named Phillips Hall in honor of Phoebe Foxcroft Phillips, widow of academy founder Samuel Phillips Jr., and their son John, who had donated funds for its construction. It was built as a four-story Federal brick structure with a symmetrical façade. Modeled after collegiate architecture at Brown, Yale, and Princeton, it included dormitory rooms for 30 students, classrooms, and a chapel. In 1870 and again in 1912, structural problems in the east wall required extensive rebuilding and loss of much of the historic fabric. In 1929 Charles Platt, mastermind of the new campus plan, removed the fourth floor, so that Foxcroft would conform to the architecture of the new buildings on the quadrangle. The original entrances with lunettes, stone lintels, and sills remain.

Bartlet Hall was built in 1821 as a second dormitory and mate to Foxcroft. Modest Federal details, including recessed entries with lunettes and paneling, a cornice with modillions, four large square chimneys, windows with multi-pane lights, and splayed brownstone lintels, survive extensive remodeling. In 1914 the building was completely gutted by fire and rebuilt. Fifteen years later, Bartlet, like Foxcroft, was lowered to harmonize with surrounding architecture. Bartlet and Foxcroft remain dormitories.

In the 1820s life in the dorms was considerably more Spartan than today. Sarah Stuart Robbins, who grew up on Andover Hill as a faculty child in the 1820s, offered this vivid picture of daily life for seminary students:

> There was no water in the buildings; the young men must bring it in their pitchers from outside. There was no steam heat; they must tend their own stoves, carrying their fuel from a wood-pile which at first was not even protected from the rain and snow, up the steep flights of stairs to their rooms. They had to make their own beds, do their own sweeping, and fill their own lamps. But there was little complaint among the theologues of eighty years ago. . . . That these hardships, which students of to-day would doubtless think severe, did no harm to those then subjected to them, is proved by the quality of the graduates sent out by Andover in those early days.

Charles Bulfinch designed Pearson Hall, the second building in Seminary Row. Similar to Bartlet Hall, this building was originally named

Pearson Hall

for its donor, William Bartlet of Newburyport, one of the founders of the seminary. It housed a sanctuary and library, as well as classrooms for the seminarians, and was known as Bartlet Chapel. It was later renamed Pearson Hall, in honor of Eliphalet Pearson, the first principal of Phillips Academy and the major force behind the seminary. The Newburyport bricks, 12-over-12 pane windows, the sandstone lintels, sills, keystones, and corner blocks are original. Bulfinch had originally stipulated marble details on all four facades. Bartlet, who had almost complete control of the construction, replaced the marble with sandstone, presumably for economy's sake. At first he had thought it might be painted white to simulate the more expensive material, but reconsidered when the building was finished.

Nothing remains of Bulfinch's interior—the building was remodeled and a clock tower added in 1875—but Sarah Stuart Robbins recalled the chapel in the 1820s:

> It was in those days divided into three stories instead of two, as now, the floors having since been shifted, and the windows of the middle story blocked up. . . . On the right, the chapel filled the lower story; and above was the library, which, with its books, portraits, and busts, was a most attractive place. The left side of the building was occupied by recitation rooms. . . . The [chapel] walls were dingy blue, the pews, gallery, and desk were yellow white. Between the windows tarnished candelabra swung out, holding long, thin tallow dips, which had a sacerdotal habit of dripping large, round, hot drops upon unsanctified heads . . . In winter a great iron stove on one side of the pulpit with

Pearson Hall classroom

pipes running around the entire chapel formed the only means of heating. Into this the sexton, who had a seat near the wood-box, on the other side of the pulpit, was continually shoving large sticks of well-seasoned wood. With the hot coals, foot-stoves were filled; and passing these stoves from one to another made the principal diversion from the service.

In 1922 Guy Lowell restored Pearson to its original appearance, with a recreated cupola, cornice, and balustrade. It was also moved back and turned 90 degrees at the south end of the Great Quadrangle, to open the vista to Samuel Phillips Hall, then under construction. Pearson Hall is now a classroom building.

4. George Washington Hall   *Charles A. Platt, 1925–1926*

On the north side of the Great Quad, Charles Platt erected his first major structure for the academy, the new administration building. The trustees chose Charles Platt over Guy Lowell, who had worked for Phillips Academy for twenty-four years, designing everything from the baseball cage to dormitories. Lowell's style was distinctly different from Platt's, a contrast made vividly apparent by the juxtaposition of Sam Phil and George Washington Hall.

The main façade of George Washington Hall, known as simply "GW" on campus, faces the Quad with a strong central pedimented pavilion that frames three entrances with lunettes. Compared to the portico of Samuel Phillips Hall, Platt's design is slim and refined. Limestone trim and tablets highlight the windows and doors of the portico, while the flanking wings are more austerely simple with unadorned windows and only limestone string courses to relieve the brick. According to *The Phillips Bulletin* of June 1925, the design was considered "Georgian Colonial of the Bulfinch period, in harmony with most of the existing Academy buildings; indeed its front gable, its entrance doors with fan lights, and its small pane windows will repeat charming features already found in Pearson Hall and [Bulfinch Hall], which were erected in 1818."

GW was designed to house offices for the principal, registrar, treasurer, and other administrators. It also provided a large auditorium, with seating for more than 1,200 people, a welcome alternative to the old Stone Chapel. Until the fall of 1926 all large events were held in Stone Chapel, often to the consternation of faculty and administrators. Sometimes these gatherings, such as those preceding the annual Andover-Exeter football game, became too indecorous for a house of worship. There was, therefore, palpable relief when another space became available. An unnamed writer articulated his appreciation in *The Phillips Bulletin.*

> . . . when . . . the chapel resounds with stormy applause for . . . the 'school gladiators,' there are those whose sensibilities are shocked. . . . when this auditorium is completed, we shall be able to keep Stone Chapel inviolate and to hold lectures, concerts, plays, moving picture shows, and other delightful school functions in a hall better adapted to their presentation and less likely to seem incongruous.

George Washington Hall

5. Chapel Cemetery *1810*

Stowe family gravestones in Chapel Cemetery

Between George Washington and Samuel Phillips Halls is the path to the Phillips Academy Cemetery. Originally called Chapel Cemetery, it was established in 1810 as a final resting-place for students, faculty, principals, and others associated with the seminary and the academy. It was enlarged in late 1920 by the Olmsted Brothers and protected by a fieldstone wall. It is now surrounded by classroom and dormitory buildings. Headstones or small monuments mark most graves. One exception is a High Gothic style marble and granite monument to Leonard Woods, Professor of Christian Theology at the seminary, who died in 1854. Also buried here are Professor Calvin Stowe and his wife Harriet Beecher Stowe, who resided in Andover for twelve years.

6. Samuel F.B. Morse Hall *Guy Lowell, 1927–1928*

Samuel F. B. Morse Hall, from Flagstaff Quadrangle

On the south side of the Great Quadrangle, next to Pearson Hall, the academy erected a new science building in 1928. Named for the inventor and artist who graduated from Phillips in 1805, Samuel F. B. Morse Hall was the last building Guy Lowell designed for Andover. After his sudden death in February 1927, his associates and successors Ralph C. Henry and Henry P. Richmond completed the project.

Nine months before his death, Lowell corresponded with Phillips Academy treasurer James C. Sawyer about some preliminary plans, advising against a "twin brother to Pearson Hall."

> A building such as we have drawn out does not try to reproduce Pearson Hall and does not try to establish an absolute balance where none can really exist. . . . What we have done is to take the space needed so as to group the various rooms in the most efficient way and we have then designed an elevation to harmonize with the style and

Guy Lowell, Study for Morse Hall from the Great Quad

the mass of the other buildings of the group. The result is that the building actually ties the whole group better together than if it were an exact repetition of the Pearson Hall type.

A small drawing of Morse Hall suggests that Lowell had in mind a richly detailed front facade, with two-story columns or pilasters and a large arched window at either end. The trustees apparently did not approve the design. In the middle of January 1927 they asked Lowell to redesign the façade, which they felt was too elaborate to harmonize with the rest of the Quad. Within days of Lowell's death, Henry and Richmond refined the elevations.

As built, Morse Hall is a three-story, rectangular brick block with a small single level wing on the west end. The otherwise smooth façade is softened by shallow arched reveals on the second floor. The granite detailing of the brick façade, double hung sash windows with multi-pane lights, wooden balustrades on outer windows, and cornice with modillions are strategic elements, allowing Morse to sit comfortably beside Pearson Hall. The academy officially appreciated the restraint of the final scheme.

> The charm of the design lies chiefly in good proportion and carefully studied fenestration. The severity of the main façade is relieved by the simple rythmic [sic] spacing of the windows and the architectural detail of the central doorway and porch. Further interest is added by the arched reveals enclosing the group of two windows on each end of the second story and in these reveals a brick pattern is introduced.

Overall the building is more restrained than Lowell's design for Samuel Phillips Hall, and more compatible with Charles Platt's Georgian revival taste. For Platt, who was advising the trustees on this project, architectural sympathy with Pearson was paramount, and the arched reveals, balustrades, and splayed lintels on the north façade all harmonize with similar nineteenth-century features on Pearson. Ironically, it was Platt who had ordered the fourth floor of Bartlet and Foxcroft removed in 1922, to bring these old Federal-era buildings into proportion with their new revivalist neighbors.

7. Flagstaff Quadrangle: Day Hall, Commons, Paul Revere Hall

Day Hall *Guy Lowell, 1910–1911*
Commons *Charles A. Platt, 1928–1930*
Paul Revere Hall *Charles A. Platt, 1928–1929*

The path between Morse and Pearson Halls leads into Flagstaff Quadrangle. Like its larger neighbor, Flagstaff was the creation of Charles Platt. In 1921, when Platt began to refocus the campus east of Main Street, Day Hall was already in place, just south of Bartlet Hall. For a time, an earlier building called the Sanhedrin, a bathhouse and laundry for seminary students, stood nearly in the center of the present quad, moved there by Platt to make room for Sam Phil. Morse and Pearson Halls provided the northern side of the quad. In 1929 Platt had the Sanhedrin demolished and added another dormitory, Paul Revere Hall, on the east. Commons, built on the south in 1930, enclosed the quad.

Guy Lowell designed Day Hall, the first of the buildings in the quadrangle. The Olmsted Brothers urged the trustees to locate this new dormitory in line with Seminary Row, so as not to distract from the older

The Sanhedrin and Blanchard House, 1922–1929

Day Hall

buildings. Designed to be compatible with Foxcroft, Pearson, and Bartlet, Day was constructed of red brick on a low granite foundation with stone trim. Granite steps lead to two entries, reflecting the original interior layout of two separate houses, divided by a firewall. Rooms for 23 boys and one instructor were laid out in each half of the building. The recessed doorways are embellished with wood trim and fluted pilasters, supporting an entablature.

In 1929 Platt sited a second dormitory, Paul Revere Hall, opposite Day Hall on the eastern end of Flagstaff Quad. Like the other buildings on the quad, Paul Revere is constructed of brick on a granite foundation. Multi-

paned, double-hung windows reinforce its Georgian revival style. The gambrel roof disguises a full fourth floor of dormitory space, lit by segmented arched dormers, keeping the building in scale with its neighbors. The front façade has a center entrance framed by a pedimented portico with pilasters. Named for the American silversmith who had engraved the official Phillips Academy

Paul Revere Hall

seal in 1782, Paul Revere Hall originally provided rooms for 60 boys and two unmarried instructors. It remains a dormitory.

Commons, designed by Charles Platt as the first central dining facility for the entire academy community, completed the quad in 1930. Its simple façade and projecting wings quietly contain Flagstaff Quad on the

Commons

south side. Platt designed a shallow run of steps leading to three double-door entries with lunettes, which are echoed in arched windows and reveals across the façade. Multi-pane sash reduce the scale of the large windows, and simple stone keystones, string courses, and a cornice relieve the plain brick walls. In 1928, just as construction for Commons began, the decision was made to put a flagpole in the center of the new quadrangle, hence the name Flagstaff Quadrangle. Platt designed its elaborate base.

8. Hardy House and Shuman Admission Center

Hardy House   *1804–1805*
Shuman Admission Center   *David P. Handlin & Associates, 2000*

Across Salem Street from the Flagstaff Quad, the Shuman Admission Center incorporates one of the academy's oldest structures with the newest. The building has a long history of renovation. In 1801 the trustees purchased a small cottage from Captain Asa Towne. By 1804 they had added a narrow gambrel roof structure, larger than the original cottage and perpendicular to it, facing Main Street. It was a vernacular eighteenth-century building: two-and-a-half stories with end chimneys and 12-over-12 pane windows.

When it was built, the house was designed to provide six identical rooms for academy boys, the first academy-owned dormitory on campus, and the new spaces were simple and serviceable. In the spring of 1806, before students could move in, Eliphalet Pearson returned to Andover with his family. The trustees made Hardy House available to him to live in while he established the theological seminary. Additional improvements had to be made for Pearson who was, after all, president of the board of trustees. The original cottage became a kitchen ell, and the interior of the "addition" was embellished with trim, paint and wallpaper. After Pearson's tenure, principal John Adams lived there with his family and several students from 1810 to 1833. Professor William Graves, who restructured the academy's science program, occupied the house for more than 40 years. During Graves' residency, Boston architect William Ralph Emerson removed the old kitchen ell and replaced it with a new colonial revival wing. The building was used as a faculty residence well into the twentieth century.

In the 1970s the school remodeled Hardy House for the Phillips Academy admission office. Yet 20 years later it was no longer adequate for the enlarged admission program. The academy decided to preserve and restore the 1804 section, demolish the rest, and build a new addition designed by Cambridge architect David P. Handlin & Associates. The new wing preserves the integrity of the older building as a distinct unit. Built over the footprint of the demolished ell, the Shuman Admission Center repeats the clapboard siding and general scale of the Hardy Wing. Windows are narrower and have larger panes than their older counterparts. As part of the restoration of Hardy House, the original front entry, which Emerson had relocated on the south façade in 1886, was returned to the front of the building. The heavily used admissions office entrance is on the other side of the addition on a new courtyard and parking area.

Shuman Admission Center and Hardy House

9. Bulfinch Hall *Asher Benjamin, 1818–1819*

Bulfinch Hall was built as the third main Academy building. Unlike the "wooden Academy," which had burned to the ground in February 1818, this "Brick Academy" was aligned with Seminary Row, but located at a distance on the opposite side of Salem Street. For many years the hall was considered the work of Boston architect Charles Bulfinch, though a recent discovery firmly attributes it to architect-builder Asher Benjamin. Historian David Chase found documentation among the treasurer's records of a $15.00 payment to Benjamin for a "Plan of Acad" in May 1818. The payment was likely for a drawing of the exterior only. The interior was closely modeled on the old Academy: three rooms on the first floor for classrooms, library, and museum, and a large hall upstairs for debates, examinations, and graduation exercises.

The Stone Academy on Chapel Avenue shared some of those functions in the 1840s and 1850s. When that structure burned during the winter of 1864, a much larger main Academy was planned at the intersection of School and Main Streets. As soon as that new building was underway in 1865, the trustees voted to convert Bulfinch Hall to a gymnasium for seminarians and academy boys. With facilities for gymnastics, bowling and boxing, the new gym opened on February 14, 1867 and was heavily used and poorly maintained for almost thirty years. In 1896 a fire of suspicious origin gutted the building completely. A photograph of the inferno was inscribed with words of Oliver Wendell Holmes, Phillips Academy Class of

Bulfinch Hall

Handwritten on image:

P. A.
Gym.
Built as
Academy Building
1818.
Burning 1 A.M
June 23,
1896.

"I, whose fresh voice yon red-faced temple knew,
What tune is left me, fit to sing to you?
-- How all comes back! the upward slanting floor,
The masters' thrones that flank the central door,
The long outstretching alleys that divide
The rows of desks that stand on either side."
                              Oliver Wendell Holmes.

Bulfinch Hall on fire, 1896

1825, who wrote "The School Boy" in 1878, celebrating his experiences at the academy. He described Bulfinch in better days:

> I, whose fresh voice you red-faced temple knew,
> What tune is left me, fit to sing to you?
> How all comes back! The upward slanting floor,
> The masters' thrones that flank the central door,
> The long outstretching alleys that divide
> The rows of desks that stand on either side.

Guy Lowell renovated the brick shell in 1902 for the school's dining hall. The main dining hall was on the first floor, with a banquet room on the second, and the kitchen and service areas in a new wing on the east. Six years after Charles Platt's new Commons building was completed, Bulfinch Hall was rehabilitated again, this time as the English Department. Perry, Shaw, & Hepburn, architects of Colonial Williamsburg, created an opulent colonial revival interior for classes, debates, and offices. The building was christened Bulfinch Hall at that time. In 1983 the narrow road leading to Bulfinch was designated as Grub Street, not a sly comment on the building's past as an eatery, but a more erudite reference to a street in eighteenth-century London frequented by writers.

Bulfinch Hall today is a record of nearly 200 years of adaptive use and renovation. Fate, practicality, and creativity have conspired to produce a building that it still graceful and vital. Of Asher Benjamin's original design, only the walls remain intact. Finely crafted of brick in Flemish bond with thin mortar joints, the façade is detailed with granite sills, lintels, foundation, and door surrounds. The main façade, facing Main Street, has a shallow three-bay pavilion, with a center entrance flanked by columns and crowned by a lunette. The secondary entrance on the north elevation has a more rusticated treatment. The window sash and roof as well as the entire interior were consumed in the fire of 1896. The restoration by Perry, Shaw, & Hepburn included a hipped roof with small domed cupola and a pediment with a distinctive elliptical window. As a whole, Bulfinch Hall is a significant example of stylish Colonial Revival design.

Between Bulfinch Hall and Main Street, the academy has erected monuments to honor the young men of Phillips Academy who have died in military service. The path from Bulfinch Hall toward Main Street passes by Borden Gymnasium and Memorial Place. Originally designed in 1901 by Peabody & Stearns of Boston, Borden has been altered repeatedly over the years as demand for physical education facilities has changed. In 1951 Eggers & Higgins were commissioned to build an extensive addition, called Memorial Gymnasium in honor of Phillips Academy alumni who had died in World War II.

Across the path, the broken columns of Memorial Place stand in poignant homage to the Phillips students lost in the Korean and Vietnam conflicts. Designed by Prentice & Chan, Ohlhausen of New York, Memorial Place was dedicated in 1994.

Borden Gymnasium

Memorial Bell Tower and Memorial Place

The Bell Tower was erected in 1923 at the corner of Salem and Main Streets, as a memorial to Phillips Academy alumni who had lost their lives in World War I. It is now a landmark, the first glimpse of Academy Hill as one approaches Andover from the south. A tower appeared in Lowell's 1919 scheme to develop the central academy campus on the other side of Main Street. Following the decision to locate Samuel Phillips Hall, the main classroom building, behind Seminary Row, it seemed appropriate to transfer the tower as well.

Donor Samuel L. Fuller, P.A. 1891, selected the site on the old militia training ground. Although the trustees had agreed not to erect any academy buildings on this revered space, a war memorial was considered a fitting addition. Troops had convened here from at least the Revolutionary War through World War I. In November 1789 President Washington passed through Andover on his way to Lexington. He met Samuel Phillips Jr. at a local tavern and reportedly visited the Phillipses at Mansion House and reviewed the Andover militia on this field. Indeed, Samuel Phillips and Washington shared some personal history; Phillips was active in revolutionary war politics, and procured supplies for the general's headquarters in Cambridge. From 1776 into the 1790s Phillips had operated a marginally successful gunpowder mill in Andover.

The bell tower is a square brick structure built over a steel frame, with a deep limestone base and an exuberant three-tier wooden spire surmounted by a weathervane. Finials abound. Typical of Lowell's work, there is a decorative, almost delicate effect in the details of finials and shutters. Fuller referred to the tower as "absolutely useless," but a form he associated with the bells of Florence, where he was stationed during the war. Now perceived as a monument, a meeting place, and a focal point, Memorial Tower was also a source of music for many years. In 1926, installation of a thirty-seven bell carillon was completed, one of the largest in the United States. Unfortunately, the interior stairway and support structure are no longer safe for the bell player to ascend to the carillon, and are awaiting restoration.

Cochran Chapel and the Addison Gallery of American Art on the Great Lawn

11. Great Lawn and Elm Arch, *circa 1820*

Directly across Salem Street from the Memorial Bell Tower, the Great Lawn extends to Chapel Avenue. This space has remained open since the academy was founded. Originally a swampy meadow in front of Seminary Row, it was gradually improved in the 1810s and 1820s. The building of Foxcroft, Pearson, and Bartlet Halls involved the creation of a terrace, which was enclosed by granite bollards linked by chain in 1821.

The Elm Arch stands in front of the former Seminary Row, where Eliphalet Pearson is said to have laid it out in the early nineteenth century. Despite some losses from Dutch Elm disease, the allée remains the lawn's defining north-south axis. The seminary library, Brechin Hall (1865), designed by Charles Cummings, once stood at the southern end of the Elm Arch, near the current site of the Armillary Sphere. Brechin was torn down in 1929 in large part because it interfered with the broad sweep across the lawn from Salem Street to Chapel Avenue.

Elm Arch

The Armillary Sphere, by American sculptor Paul Manship (1885–1966), sits toward the southern end of the Lawn. Installed in the early 1930s, it was designed to be a "symbol of the world," according to Manship—humanity at the center of the celestial universe. The four elements—earth, wind, fire and water—are represented, as are the astrological signs of the year. The axis of the sphere is fixed at 42° 30', the angle of the earth at Andover, and points due north, so the axis shaft casts a shadow on the equatorial belt, indicating the time of day. At noon of each day, the shadow is directly south. The Armillary Sphere originally occupied the space in front

Armillary Sphere

of Samuel Phillips Hall, at the top of the Vista. It was moved almost immediately to its present location at the southern end of the Elm Walk.

12. Oliver Wendell Holmes Library   *Charles A. Platt, 1928–1929*

In 1928, Platt designed the Oliver Wendell Holmes Library to house the burgeoning collection of books accumulated by the academy. The library had outgrown Brechin Hall, which it had inherited from the seminary, and Platt wanted to eliminate Brechin as part of his grand scheme for the central campus. Platt located the new library well forward of Seminary Row facing Main Street. At the time, he had designated a site at the opposite end of the Great Lawn for a new chapel, to replace Cummings & Sears' Gothic Stone Chapel. The library and the chapel were to serve as vanguards to the central campus, anchoring both ends of the Lawn and framing first Foxcroft and Bartlet, and ultimately Samuel Phillips Hall.

The library's original main façade presides over the southern lawn. The two-story limestone portico supported by columns and surmounted by a pediment is, by now, a familiar feature on the academy campus. Settled fairly low on a granite foundation with only a handful of steps to the entrance, the understated domestic scale of Platt's library was repeated in the Commons, which he completed the following year. The two-story building with hipped roof and expansive skylights is virtually intact. Constructed of brick, with stone details and double hung wood sash, it is consistent with the vocabulary chosen by Platt, and Guy Lowell before him, to harmonize with the original colonial architecture of Seminary Row.

Two reading rooms and the central hall also remain as Platt intended and are open to the public. Georgian style woodwork lines both the reference study area known as the Garver Reading Room and the less formal Freeman Room. On one wall of the Freeman Room is a mural painted by Stuart Travis depicting the history of the academy overlaid on a map of Andover as it appeared in 1830. Originally, the second floor housed seminar rooms and the book delivery area, with access to five levels of stacks.

In 1959 James S. Copley, P.A. 1935, donated funds for a new library wing to house materials for an intensive American history course, as part of a comprehensive building campaign called The Andover Program. A new reading room provided space for a reserve system, relieving some of the overcrowding in the Garver Room, as well as several dozen study carrels. Designed by Benjamin Thompson of The Architects Collaborative in Cambridge, the Copley Wing was essentially a glass structure, attached to the older brick building without disturbing it. With this addition, the main entrance shifted to the new wing, at the back of Platt's building, just off the Flagstaff Quad.

Thirty years later, the Copley Wing was entirely replaced by a more ambitious addition, designed by Shepley, Bulfinch, Richardson & Abbot. Expanded facilities for computer access, open stacks, administrative offices, and a state of the art computer center were fully integrated into the original library. Platt's reading rooms remain popular with students and are used on a daily basis. With the main entrance on the west, however, Platt's elegant front façade is now primarily ceremonial.

Oliver Wendell Holmes Library

Addison Gallery of American Art

13. Addison Gallery of American Art   *Charles A. Platt, 1929–1931*

Open to the public, 10 am to 5 pm Tuesday through Saturday, 1 pm to 5 pm Sunday; closed major holidays and the month of August.

As the library was being completed, Platt was involved with a plan for the northern end of the Great Lawn. A new chapel, he thought, should replace the outdated Stone Chapel and balance the library.

By summer 1928, the idea of a free-standing Phillips Academy art museum had superseded the original plan for gallery space on the second floor of the library. Suddenly, a new building site was needed. Platt chose the chapel site, or rather just south of it, for the Addison Gallery of American Art. The new chapel would be relocated across Chapel Avenue near the corner of Main Street. As architect of the Corcoran Gallery addition and the Freer Gallery, both in Washington, Platt had considerable experience planning art museums when he began the task of designing one for the academy. His plan for the Lyman Allen Museum in New London, Connecticut, completed in 1930, is virtually the same as the Addison's. Although he had toyed with a Renaissance palazzo design, he finally decided on an elegant colonial revival temple of brick, set high on a granite foundation with a double flight of broad stairs. Doric columns support a central portico with pediment above. A massive copper lantern hangs inside the recessed porch above bronze and glass doors. The entry is flanked by two large multi-light windows with a fanlight above. Two pairs of blind windows on each story provide balance and rhythm to the façade. Above a simple cornice is a hip roof of glass and metal.

The interior of the museum is virtually intact. A small vestibule leads to an octagonal lobby with limestone walls, patterned marble floor, and sumptuous plasterwork on a shallow domed ceiling. In the center is a

fountain by Paul Manship, commissioned by Platt for this room. Although some gallery spaces have been modified for offices on the first floor, the Platt-designed scale and details have been preserved. The second floor galleries, accessible by an elegant marble staircase, remain as Platt designed them. The main gallery, with its soaring glass ceiling and deep cove molding, painted by Sol LeWitt in 1993, is countered by four more intimate galleries. Doorways with molded marble surrounds are placed asymmetrically in the gallery walls to create subtle shifts in sight lines and maximize visual flow.

Addison Gallery of American Art

The museum opened in May 1931 as the Addison Gallery of American Art, named for Keturah Addison Cobb, a family friend of Thomas Cochran, P.A. 1890. The building, the museum's endowment, and the core collection were gifts of Cochran, the school's greatest benefactor and major supporter of Charles Platt. Since its opening, the Addison has become a highly respected art museum, known nationally and internationally for its collection of American art. In a virtually unique association with a secondary school, it strives to be both an essential part of the academy's humanities curriculum and a cultural resource for local communities.

Diagonally across Chapel Avenue is Cochran Chapel, completed in 1932. Originally planned for the site of the Addison Gallery, next to the old Stone Chapel, Cochran Chapel was the final element of Platt's central campus. When the new chapel was relocated to Chapel Avenue, several buildings stood in Platt's way. (The Teachers' Seminary had been located on the corner of Chapel and Main, but burned down in 1864.) He reorganized the entire street. A private house facing Wheeler Street was relocated. Samaritan House, where headmaster Alfred Stearns lived, was moved to School Street. Bartlet Street, which at the time intersected Chapel Avenue,

Cochran Chapel

also interfered with Platt's plans. He had the academy negotiate with the town to close Bartlet at Wheeler Street. Despite some vocal objections from faculty and administration that the whole process was moving too quickly and that the historic buildings were all being displaced from the campus, Platt steamed ahead.

Cochran Chapel

On its new site, Platt adjusted his chapel to align with the Memorial Bell Tower, instead of simply parallel Main Street, to reinforce the north-south axis of the lawn. He even stipulated that a gap should be made in the stone wall along Chapel Avenue to open the view of the chapel from the lawn. The space is now overgrown with shrubbery.

The Chapel marked the end of the highly productive Cochran-Platt partnership. Platt died in 1933. Cochran passed away in 1936 after a long illness. The May 1932 dedication of Cochran Chapel, named for the patron's parents, was the last time Thomas Cochran visited Phillips Academy.

Like many other Platt buildings on campus, the Chapel is a Georgian revival brick, granite, and limestone structure. The central portico with three tall arched openings and applied stone pilasters rests on a broad flight of granite steps. Three arched doorways with fanlights repeat the rhythm. The side elevations have seven two-story arched windows, flanked by pairs of round windows. The architect's admiration for American colonial design is evident. According to Platt historian Keith Morgan, the portico was modeled on the Lancaster, Massachusetts meeting house, designed in 1817 by Charles Bulfinch. Similarly, the 200-foot steeple with square brick base punctuated by round windows on all four sides, two lanterns, and an octagonal copper-sheathed spire, is thought to be based on Philip Hooker's Second Presbyterian Church in Albany.

In contrast to its colonial shell, the interior is surprisingly opulent. The vestibule is an elegant three-part space with dark green and white marble tile floor. The nave is filled with light from immense clear glass windows. (Platt forbade the use of stained glass!) Two-story fluted columns support arcades which define the side aisles. Sheathed entirely in carved, fumed oak with a painted, coffered barrel vault ceiling, the sanctuary looks more to Christopher Wren than to Bulfinch. Pairs of carved cherubs gaze down benignly from the column capitals. The paneled organ screen with choir loft above is richly detailed.

Numerous minor renovations were completed in the 1970s and 1980s. The original stationary pulpit was removed in 1990 to accommodate choral and theatrical uses of the building. In 1999 a small organ balcony at the back of the sanctuary was expanded by Ann Beha & Associates of Boston, making space for the entire student body and faculty to assemble for weekly all-school meetings. This highly sensitive renovation was so successful that many visitors are unable to distinguish new elements from old. The academy shares this extraordinary space with the local community through public programs and services.

15. Andover Inn *Bottomley, Wagner & White, 1929–1930*

The Andover Inn

Another of Platt's challenges on Chapel Avenue was the Andover Inn, or the Phillips Inn as it was called until 1940. It originally consisted of an old stone house, the former residence of Harriet Beecher Stowe and her husband, and a huge wooden addition from the 1890s. As late as February 1929, plans were underway to demolish the inn's wooden ell and build two new wings, faced with granite to harmonize with Stowe House. Soon thereafter, however, the school chose to move the old stone building to Bartlet Street and build an entirely new inn on the original site.

Designed by Sidney Wagner of Bottomley, Wagner & White, with Charles Platt as supervising architect, the Georgian style inn contains 23 guestrooms on three stories. A recessed porch with columns fronts the main façade, which projects out from two flanking wings. Multi-pane double hung windows and French doors help maintain the domestic scale of the building. The slate gambrel roof has dormers and eyebrow windows to light the third floor rooms. A two-story wing extends back from the left rear of the building, framing a yard that overlooks Rabbit Pond. A stone wall once enclosed an elaborate garden designed by Olmsted Brothers and Charles Platt.

On the interior, the main lobby and two large dining rooms retain Georgian revival woodwork, enhancing the relaxed atmosphere of a traditional New England inn. Although owned by Phillips Academy, the inn has always been independently managed. As it has throughout its history, today the inn provides lodging for returning alumni and parents of academy students, as well as visitors to the regional community.

16. Stowe House *1824 or 1828*

On the northern end of the parking lot between the Andover Inn and Cochran Chapel is Stowe House, now a dormitory for academy students. In the 1820s, Professor Moses Stuart persuaded the Andover Theological Seminary to build a fieldstone shell with a gambrel roof as a workshop for students. Highly innovative at the time, the plan was to provide exercise for theological students, exercise that consisted of practical carpentry. Students made all kinds of wooden items for sale, including for a time, coffins. Even as a child Sarah Stuart Robbins felt empathy for the hapless theologues,

Stowe House

There were pale, puzzled, weary faces, bending over corners that wouldn't fit, and over boards that were too long or too short, too narrow or too wide. There were failures to hit nails on the head; there was dulling of saws, breaking of hatchets, and rasping of files;—oh, the ignorance and incompatibility are as funny to remember as they must have been hard to bear. To the participants there was nothing amusing about the scene. Each man was as solemn as if the coffin he was making were his own.

After the workshop was disbanded, the stone house was allowed to collect rubbish and for a while was equipped as a gymnasium for both seminary and academy students. It was vacant in 1852 when Harriet Beecher Stowe arrived in Andover with her husband, Calvin E. Stowe, who was to teach at the seminary. She had just published *Uncle Tom's Cabin* and her presence caused quite a stir on the hill. Mrs. Stowe convinced the seminary to transform the old stone workshop into a comfortable residence. A bit more daring than most seminary wives, she entertained guests with tableaux and charades, put up a Christmas tree and distributed gifts—in the days when Christmas was not condoned as a holiday in conservative New England—and was even suspected of attending the theater in Boston. The Stowes remained in Andover for twelve years, during which time Mrs. Stowe wrote three books in her first-floor study: *Dred, The Pearl of Orr's Island,* and *The Minister's Wooing.* The Stowes apparently had fond memories of Andover, for their graves lie in the old Chapel Cemetery near that of their teenaged son.

In addition to the extensive remodeling Mrs. Stowe must have done on the interior, she added a lovely Italianate porch and wooden fence that survived until at least 1885. After the Stowes left Andover, the seminary converted the house into a dormitory. A fire in July 1887 extensively damaged the building, and soon thereafter it was renovated again as the Phillips Inn, replacing the former Mansion House which had been destroyed by fire that fall. In 1893, a huge wooden addition on the east side provided additional space for inn patrons. This addition, as well as Mrs. Stowe's porch, was demolished when Charles Platt moved the building to Bartlet Street. What remains is essentially a product of the colonial revival expansion of the campus.

17. Graham House *Codman & Despradelle, 1915*

Stephen Codman and Désiré Despradelle produced some of the most innovative buildings in Boston in the early 1900s, including the Berkeley Building and the Peter Bent Brigham Hospital in Boston. Despradelle taught at the Massachusetts Institute of Technology where Guy Lowell had been one of his students. Despradelle had died in 1912, well before Graham House was designed, but Codman continued to use the firm's name.

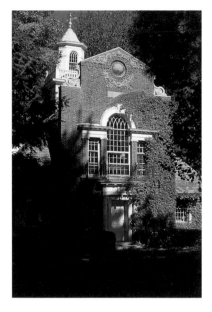

Graham House

Graham House, on Wheeler Street, is a delightful architectural confection. It remains essentially as it was built, with the only alteration being three windows added on the west side. The entire exterior design is composed around the three-story gable end of the front façade. The ground level entrance is flanked by columns that support a deep entablature. Above the entry is a massive Palladian window, with elaborate Renaissance motifs in copper high in the peak of the gable. The steeply pitched roof with green slate shingles is a major decorative feature, as is the charming cupola. The elements are all Georgian revival, but unlike most of the twentieth-century buildings on campus, they are assembled to create a highly idiosyncratic building.

Graham House was built originally as the headquarters of AUV (Auctoritas, Unitas, Veritas), one of Phillips Academy's secret societies, social fraternities modeled after those at Yale. In 1950, after the societies were officially banned on campus, the house was named after Professor John Chandler Graham and converted to office space. It is used today by the Counseling Center.

Faculty Row

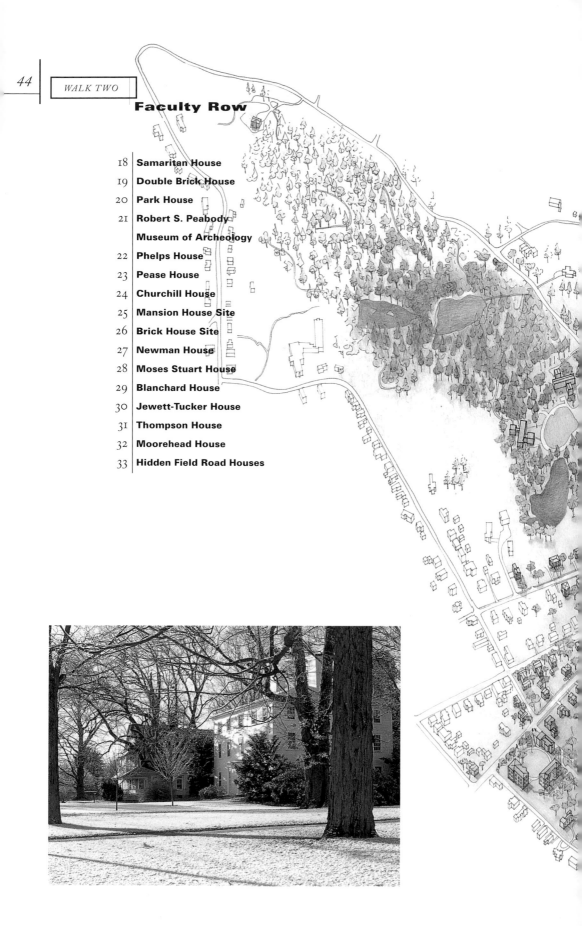

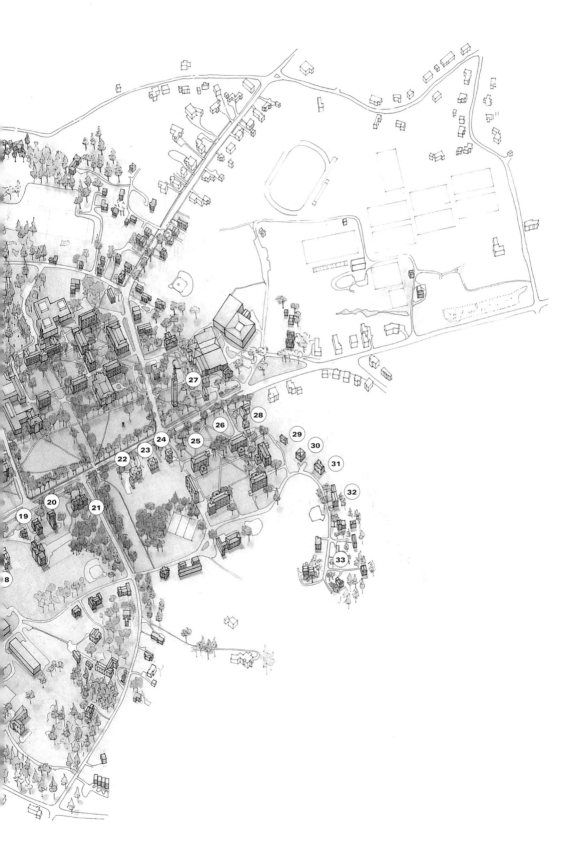

Seminary Faculty Houses

On the west side of Main Street, from School Street to Hidden Field Road, is a stretch of houses known for many years as Faculty Row. In 1909 Phillips Academy acquired these houses, built in the early nineteenth century for the professors of the Andover Theological Seminary, with all the rest of the seminary's property on the east side. They still retain their domestic character, though some are now small dormitories for academy students.

Founded in 1808 to train Calvinist ministers and missionaries, the theological seminary needed to attract the major theologians of the day. Planning for faculty housing began as soon as the first seminary building was underway. Of college and preparatory schools, Andover was unique in providing faculty housing at the school's expense and so close to campus. When Leonard Woods was recruited by the seminary in 1807 he suggested, "If houses could be built by the trustees for the professors it would add to the beauty of the seminary, and to the convenience of the professors, and be an alluring circumstance to those who shall be appointed from time to time."

Five houses were built for seminary faculty between 1810 and 1835: Double Brick, Park, Phelps, Pease, and Moses Stuart Houses. William Bartlet of Newburyport, the seminary's most generous supporter, funded all five. (During this period Bartlet also paid for Pearson and Bartlet Halls, and possibly the stone shell that became Stowe House, all on the east side of Main Street.) All five remain in their original locations. Very different in style, they were built for individual faculty members to their specific needs and expectations. Leonard Woods wrote to the trustees after his house, now known as Pease, was finished: "The neat simplicity of the style in which the work is done exactly corresponds with my wishes [and] the commodiousness of the building exceeds my highest anticipation."

At this time, the "road to the meeting house" was a crooked path in front of Faculty Row, west of and roughly parallel to what is now Main, then following School Street to South Church. In the 1790s Samuel Phillips straightened it a bit. In 1804–1806 his son John was one of the primary developers of the Essex Turnpike, a new road laid out next to the old one, built as an investment for shareholders. For many years after, two roads ran through campus, a fast lane and a slow lane, so to speak, with a tree-lined mall between. The turnpike opened Andover to the stage line from Boston. The coach stopped just at the top of Academy Hill, letting passengers on and off in front of Samuel Phillips' Mansion House. The twentieth-century merge of the two roads into one thoroughfare accounts for the extra wide section of Main Street between Double Brick and Moses Stuart.

At the same time, the trustees, most notably treasurer Samuel Farrar, systematically purchased nearby property as it came on the market, ensuring control of the immediate campus. Farrar effectively created a buffer

Mansion House, 1880s

zone to protect the schools from infringement by, as he wrote, "little houses
and shops and all sorts of nuisances right in our midst." Other houses were
built along Main Street as the faculty grew. Farrar himself built a residence
and office on Main Street in 1811. Tucker and Churchill, Queen Anne
Victorian shingle style homes, appeared in the 1880s.

   The Faculty Row we know today has endured significant changes
since Bartlet first built it. In the late nineteenth and early twentieth cen-
turies, old Faculty Row was modified to meet increased demand for housing
and to welcome new opportunities for growth. In the 1920s Charles Platt
moved Tucker to Hidden Field Road to open The Vista. A decade later,
Perry, Shaw, & Hepburn created a new neighborhood of faculty houses at
the end of Hidden Field Road, winding behind the West Campus. At the
northern end of Faculty Row, Guy Lowell built the Robert S. Peabody
Museum of Archaeology in 1902, opening a new field of study for the academy. Today, the expanded Faculty Row represents more than 125 years of
American architecture—from the classical outlines of the colonial houses to
the picturesque Queen Anne residences of the 1880s.

   Although many of the early structures remain on their original
foundations, the west side was no more immune to demolition and moving
of buildings than the east side was. Fire claimed the most extravagant house
on the hill, Mansion House, in 1887. The site is still open, a broad lawn in
front of the West Quad dormitories. Other buildings have been moved and
replaced, remodeled and restored, as fate or changing needs dictated.

Samaritan House

18. Samaritan House *1824*

The very first building on this tour is a transplant. Samaritan House was moved to the intersection of Main and School Streets in 1929. It started out on Chapel Avenue, where Cochran Chapel now stands.

In 1817, the Samaritan Female Society of Andover and Vicinity was established to care for seminary and academy students who were ill, particularly those who could not afford medical attention. With a loan from Samuel Farrar, the ladies built Samaritan House as an infirmary. Here students were offered free "rooms, bedding, furniture, fuel, diet, medicine, nurses, physicians, necessaries and comforts as may be requisite and proper for their respective cases." Samaritan House operated as an infirmary for only a few years, presumably due to its tenuous financial situation, and then became a faculty home. It was the residence of the academy principal for nearly thirty years.

Samaritan House is typical of the three-story Federal residential buildings constructed in Andover: center entrance, symmetrical façade with double hung six over six windows and louvered shutters, tall end chimneys, cornice with modillions, and hipped roof. The highly ornate portico, although an authentic Federal period feature, is not original to this house. This elegant porch, complete with Corinthian columns, full entablature, and balustrade capped by urns, was fastened onto Samaritan during the summer of 1919. Taken from an unknown house, it is far more elaborate than what had been typically designed for the original seminary residences.

Just who added this flourish is unknown. The most likely candidate is Guy Lowell, whose 1911 design for the president's house at Harvard University was very similar to the remodeled Samaritan. He had added side porches to Samaritan in 1905. (They were demolished in preparation for the move from Chapel Avenue to School Street.) Lowell also made extensive interior renovations which gave the house new grandeur, appropriate for the head of Phillips Academy. Lowell replaced the staircase with one of larger scale. He added three arches to the central hall, opened up the double parlors, and installed a bay window. Lowell's affinity for decorative detail may have led him to install a grand new entrance as well. Ironically, Samaritan House was used as the headmaster's house for only four more years after moving. In 1933, a new headmaster, Claude Fuess, took over Phelps House as his home.

19. Double Brick House *William Sparrell, 1829*

Looking very much like a detached city row house, Double Brick was originally built to house academy students. In fact, William Sparrell made something of a specialty of row houses in Boston. Later than many of the houses on Faculty Row, Double Brick is an example of transitional Federal to Greek revival style structures that were common in urban areas of Massachusetts. The basic gable roof design with end chimneys is Federal in style, but the double recessed entry framed with granite piers and lintels is a Greek revival feature.

Double Brick House

Samuel Farrar financed Double Brick in 1829 through a fund he had established personally. (He called it the "Prize Fund" though no prizes were ever distributed.) About 1833, the building was transferred to the seminary, and Farrar turned his attention to building two rows of more modest three-story dormitories that would be called English Commons, for students of the Teachers' Seminary, and Latin Commons, for academy scholars. Interestingly, those wooden dormitories, built in 1833–1834, had gabled roofs and trabeated entrances similar to Double Brick. (The term "commons" was used somewhat interchangeably on Academy Hill. It might mean the place where students ate, i.e. "boarding in commons," or it might be applied to a dwelling place, such as English and Latin Commons. The context is the only means of deciphering the difference between what we might call today "room" versus "board.") Students who lived in Double Brick paid rent for their rooms to the academy, just as they would to any other landlord. They paid for meals, their "board," separately. Double Brick tenants probably ate at Judge Phillips' farm, just up Main Street.

The trustees' minutes note that Double Brick was to be rented for the benefit of Farrar's Prize fund. From 1837 to 1892, Double Brick was the residence of principals of Phillips Academy, including Cecil Bancroft who requested some improvements to his kitchen and bathroom in 1880. He described the tortuous route undertaken many times daily by his wife:

> . . . sink and water are now so placed . . . that from stove and boilers to pump and sink requires crossing the kitchen and a corner of the entry, the passage of two doorways, ascending a mongrel step, avoiding a projecting stair, and walking halfway across the sink room.

A trustee committee authorized the necessary renovations.

20. Park House *1833–1834*

Like Double Brick, Park House is more town than country house. Constructed of an unusually dark red brick, probably from the Newburyport brickyards, it cost $5,000 to build in the 1830s. William Bartlet, the seminary's most generous benefactor, erected the house at his own expense to attract Professor Thomas Skinner to the faculty. The trustees probably considered a fine brick Greek revival home more compelling than a wooden one. Nevertheless, Professor Skinner taught at the seminary for only three years. In 1836 Edwards Amasa Park, one of the most important religious thinkers in nineteenth-century America, joined the faculty as Professor of Sacred Rhetoric. He remained at the seminary, living in this house, until his death sixty-four years later. His daughter Agnes lived there until 1922, renting rooms to academy students. Park House is now a faculty residence.

Park House

A handsome Greek revival design, Park House has a recessed center entry with sidelights, gable end chimneys, and six-over-six pane windows with louvered shutters. The brick walls are set with very thin joints, detailed by sandstone window trim, and granite foundation and steps. The interior has remained remarkably intact, with much original Greek revival woodwork.

21. Robert S. Peabody Museum of Archaeology

Guy Lowell, Boston 1901–1903

MUSEUM OPEN: 12pm to 5 pm Tuesday–Saturday, closed Sunday–Monday and the month of August. Admission: free.

The corner of Main and Phillips Streets illustrates just how far the trustees and their architects and landscape architects would go to ensure that the campus made the best possible impression. It was here that Samuel Phillips had opened the first Academy in a remodeled carpenter's shop in 1778. In 1802, six years after the second Academy was built on the southeast corner of the Great Lawn, the old shop was sold for $30 and carted off. In 1811 Samuel Farrar began to build his own house on this corner site, with a separate building for his tiny office. Seventy years later, the site was selected for the residence of the elocution teacher, John Wesley Churchill. Apparently the lot was prime real estate, but Farrar House was too old-fashioned to entice this professor. Farrar was moved down Phillips Street, where it is today, and Churchill House took its place. In 1901 the lot was

Robert S. Peabody Museum of Archaeology

appropriated for the new archaeology museum. Churchill House moved south up Main Street to its present location. This single site served four different buildings in less than 125 years, setting an early precedent for the wholesale relocation of buildings, which became standard practice during Charles Platt's tenure as campus architect in the 1920s. In 1930, a plan was drawn up by the architectural historian Fiske Kimball to "restore" Faculty Row by, among other things, moving the Peabody Museum to one of three less visible locations, and returning Farrar to its original site. Kimball's plan was never realized.

Robert Singleton Peabody, valedictorian of the Phillips Academy class of 1857, and the nephew of George Peabody, the noted philanthropist who established an anthropology museum at Harvard, founded the museum. By 1899 Robert Peabody had amassed a personal collection of 40,000 archaeological artifacts from Native American sites. He planned to follow his uncle's lead and donate his collection to Harvard, but at the last minute he changed his mind, and offered it instead to the academy.

Peabody provided $150,000 to establish a museum, hire a curator and any other necessary staff, and create a department of archaeology at Phillips Academy, allied with but separate from the academy itself. He hoped that his museum would attract boys to the archaeology field, and would also provide a space for social gatherings. Although the school was in great need of more basic facilities, particularly dormitory space, the trustees could not turn down this generous gift and gratefully accepted.

The Peabody Museum was Guy Lowell's first commission for Phillips Academy. The design included all the classic features of Lowell's Ecôle des Beaux-Arts and Massachusetts Institute of Technology training.

The red brick façade was embellished with richly detailed stone trim around the entrance pavilion and the central window with balcony on the second floor, as well as brick quoins, belt courses, and arches. The tall round arched windows have been replaced with shorter versions to accommodate interior exhibit spaces.

As was typical of the finest public museums of the period, the interior of the Peabody was intended to be part of the educational experience. While the artifacts represented what was considered then the primitive culture of Native Americans, the classical architectural setting reminded visitors of the highest achievements of western civilization. The building is laid out in a simple plan of a hall and staircase flanked by large exhibit rooms. As originally built, Lowell's design included columns *in antis* between the entrance hall and the stairs. Although subsequent renovations have somewhat diminished the original space, the entry still retains the grandeur Lowell intended. The two exhibit halls on the first floor are also intact, although partitions have been added for exhibits. Original woodwork, including floor to ceiling classical moldings, have been obscured by modern tiles.

At the head of the stairs on the second floor is a landing large enough to be considered a second grand entryway for the two galleries on either side. The original coffered ceiling has been reduced in size by a modern partition. The library retains its original oak woodwork, but the ceiling has been lowered by acoustical tiles.

It was extremely unusual for a preparatory school to have its own department of archaeology with international connections, and a building to house a major collection. From the start the museum found it difficult to reconcile fieldwork and research with classroom teaching. Curator Dr. Warren K. Moorehead was frequently away on excavations, far from Andover. And while only a handful of academy students were intimately involved with the Peabody in the early years, they were offered a unique opportunity to join excavations in Maine, Georgia, and New Mexico, an experience usually available only to college and graduate students.

Perhaps in an attempt to ameliorate the isolation of the Peabody from the daily lives of the boys, two rooms on the second floor became a kind of informal annex to the library in the main Academy building. One room was reserved for open stacks, the other was furnished as a reading room, with newspapers, periodicals, and contemporary literature. In 1912 the Phillips Union moved into the museum's basement, which included an informal restaurant with a soda fountain and grille, and, not coincidentally, offered an alternative to shops in Andover Village—yet here under the watchful eye of faculty and administrators. The other end of the basement was given over to a reading room, where the older boys were allowed to smoke while reading newspapers and magazines. Above all, the sense of autonomy engendered by this student-run space had great appeal. As one anonymous student at the time wrote in *The Phillips Bulletin*, "The fact

Tucker and Churchill Houses, separated by Phillips Street, 1882 to 1901

that the students themselves are primarily responsible for the establishment of the Union argues strongly for its ultimate and complete success."
Unfortunately, only three years later, the museum was so pressed for
space that it had to reclaim the basement from the Phillips Union, but not
before an entirely new building, devoted to student activities, was erected
next door.

   Today the Peabody is a highly regarded museum and a leader in
the repatriation of Native American cultural artifacts. Like the Addison
Gallery of American Art, the Peabody serves both the public and the Phillips
Academy community.

   In 1915 the Peabody trust fund was used to construct Peabody
House, the new student union, directly behind the Peabody Museum of
Archaeology and facing Phillips Street. Guy Lowell designed this neighbor
of the museum, which opened in the fall of 1915, with the hope that it
would become "a center of undergraduate life in the Academy." For many
years, Peabody House provided a casual gathering place where students
could eat and talk in the downstairs grille, enjoy music and games in the
main first floor space, or hold club meetings and other special events in
smaller rooms on the second floor. In 1981 Peabody House was severely
damaged by fire and demolished.

   On the southwestern corner of Main and Phillips Streets, Samuel
Phillips Jr. built a large Federal style house and barn as an investment property for the academy around 1796. Although he and his wife Phoebe never
lived there, the property was generally known as Judge Phillips' farm, or
simply "the old farmhouse." A long line of outbuildings extended behind
the house down Phillips Street, "like the tail to a comet." Phillips leased the
property for thirty years, beginning in 1796, and various tenants operated it
as a country store and dairy farm, supplying milk to the academy. In 1818,
after the second academy building burned to the ground, classes were held
in the farmhouse for several months. In the 1830s it was also one of the
central dining houses or "commons," providing meals to academy boys. In

1880 the main house of Judge Phillips' farm was moved off campus to make room for Tucker House. For almost 20 years, Tucker and Churchill Houses reigned over the intersection of Phillips and Main Streets like two fine Victorian ladies. In 1929 Tucker House was relocated to Hidden Field Road to open the Vista from Samuel Phillips Hall west toward the New Hampshire hills. Although that view is now overgrown, the sight in the opposite direction, across the Great Lawn toward the old seminary buildings and Sam Phil is still impressive.

22. Phelps House *attributed to Peter Banner, 1809–1810*

Phelps House is perhaps the best example on campus of a house being tailored to a specific client. Reverend Edward Dorr Griffin was a prominent orator and preacher in Newark, New Jersey, and a theologian the trustees very much wanted to enlist for their new seminary. A nineteenth-century Andover historian quoted Daniel Webster's evaluation of Griffin's passionate preaching style, "If you are going the same way with the lightning, it won't hurt you; if not, you had better keep out of its way." The trustees recruited Griffin as their first Bartlet Professor of Pulpit Eloquence. Griffin reportedly was appointed in 1808 but did not arrive in Andover until 1809. He was reluctant to give up city life and the celebrity of his pulpit. At the same time, the minister was being pursued by the Park Street Church in Boston, a bastion of orthodoxy in a city where most Congregational churches had become Unitarian. Park Street needed a minister of Griffin's

Phelps House

stature. Griffin believed he could manage both Boston and Andover. The trustees believed he was "worth having on any terms."

No expense was spared in building what Griffin considered an appropriate house. William Bartlet not only endowed Griffin's position at the seminary but also paid for his new residence on Faculty Row. An apocryphal story is frequently told about Griffin's immoderate taste. He reportedly selected expensive, $1.00-per-roll, wallpaper for his parlor, and when some minor objections were raised over the extravagance, Griffin spitefully ordered the paperhangers to paste ordinary 25¢ paper over it.

By the time the house was finished in 1810, Dr. Griffin had resigned from the seminary; the commute between Andover and Boston proved to be too great a burden. It is not clear that he ever lived in his elegant house. Perhaps Andover's trustees felt a twinge of unChristian satisfaction when they heard that Dr. Griffin stayed at Park Street Church only five years before returning to his native Newark.

Other faculty members made Phelps House their home through the nineteenth century. Dr. Ebenezer Porter lived there when he was involved in founding the American Board of Foreign Missions and the American Temperance Society. Dr. Justin Edwards followed him, during which time he created such important periodicals as the *Boston Reporter* and publications of the American Tract Society. Between 1848 and 1879 Austin Phelps, Professor of Sacred Rhetoric and a prominent religious thinker of his day, lived in the house that is now named for him. His daughter, novelist Elizabeth Stuart Phelps Ward, wrote in the garden's summerhouse. Since 1933 Phelps House, the most elegant house on Faculty Row, has been the official residence of the Phillips Academy Head of School.

Phelps House may have been designed by English-born Boston architect Peter Banner, the architect of Elmwood, a similar house in Roxbury, as well as Park Street Church, where Dr. Griffin preached. Phelps House's central two-story block is framed by one-story wings. All three sections have low-pitched hip roofs with balustrades. The central entrance has sidelights and a lunette with leaded glass. Above is a portico with columns supporting an entablature. The principal elevation of the central block has flush board siding and the first floor windows are surmounted by blind arches. The use of flushboarding was a typical treatment, intended to suggest masonry construction. In 1994 the academy restored Phelps House to its original paint color, with the research assistance of the Society for the Preservation of New England Antiquities.

Pease House

23. Pease House *1815–1816*

In striking contrast to Phelps House, Pease is a typical three-story Federal house. The overall form is characteristic of residences found in coastal communities. Probably because it was built in rural Andover, Pease House is less elaborate in its details than its cosmopolitan cousins. A large square block with low, hipped roof, it has a symmetrical façade with a central entrance. The front portico is an accurate reconstruction of the original. In 1908 Pease was remembered as a "box like building, very square and plain. In the old days it was without blinds." It has been painted yellow since 1916. The porch and sleeping porch on the south side are early-twentieth-century additions.

Pease House was built for Leonard Woods, a kind and gentle man, and well-respected theologian. The grateful professor remarked to his patron, William Bartlet, that his residence was exactly what he wanted. He was a devoted teacher, yet even more devoted to his family. For many years he cared for his invalid wife, pulling her in a chair-wagon around campus.

> Wrapping the shawls around his little, pale wife so that no wind from the bleak Andover heavens could visit her too roughly, and seating her carefully and easily in the cushioned chair, he drew her over the graveled sidewalks with a minute attention to the spots upon which the wheels could run most smoothly. When the day was hot, he sought the deepest shadows thrown by the large elms.

Churchill House, 1880s

24. Churchill House   *Edgar Allen Poe Newcomb, 1882*

This outstanding Queen Anne house is largely intact, with important decorative features on each elevation. A variety of surface treatments, including clapboards, patterned shingles, and half-timbering, multiple porches
with turned posts, paneled chimneys and several sizes of windows, all con-
firm the eye of a talented Boston architect who was familiar with the latest
fashions. While Newcomb and other designers built many Queen Anne
style houses in Boston, Newton, and Brookline, few survive in as untouched
state as this one. Its ornamentation and asymmetrical plan made it one of
the showplaces of Andover in the late nineteenth century. A year before, in
1881, Newcomb had designed the Sanhedrin, a small brick laundry and
bathhouse behind Pearson Hall. [see Walk One: The Central Campus]

     Churchill House was built for John Wesley Churchill, Professor of
Elocution in the seminary. A friend of academy principal Cecil Bancroft,
Churchill also sometimes taught at Phillips and Abbot Academies. Churchill
House was built at the corner of Phillips and Main Streets, and was moved
south in 1901 when the school designated the Robert S. Peabody Museum
of Archaeology for that site.

25. Mansion House Site   *1782; demolished*

In 1782, only four years after founding the academy, Samuel Phillips built a grand new house for his family on what is now an open lawn opposite the Memorial Bell Tower. A Federal three-story square house with heavy doors on wrought iron hinges, and some sixty-two windows, Mansion House was the largest and most impressive dwelling on Academy Hill. For a century, it stood as a landmark of both the school and the town. The entire Andover community gathered for the raising of the frame in 1782:

> . . . stores and schools were closed, and men, women, and children gathered on the training-field in front of the foundations. That sturdy veteran, Jonathan French, offered a prayer, and then everybody seized 'ropes and pikes' to hoist the scaffolding into place. Cheer upon cheer rang out as the final successful pull was taken, and the weary laborers sought refreshment in the huge tubs of punch which had been provided by the thoughtful owner.

Samuel Phillips was a prosperous businessman who also had a long career in Massachusetts politics. He and his wife frequently entertained friends and colleagues in a style far more grand than at the other households on Academy Hill. According to one source, their rooms were generously sized and furnished with "broad open fireplaces, wide window-seats, fine paneling and wainscoting, rich mirrors, and ponderous doors on heavy hinges." Silver and fine linens were used on the dinner table. Phoebe Foxcroft Phillips dressed in satin, silk, and lace. "Madam" Phillips reportedly hosted George Washington for tea at Mansion House during his Andover visit in 1789, just before her husband accompanied the president to Lexington.

Moses Stuart, Brick, and Mansion Houses before 1887

After Samuel's death in 1802 Phoebe lived on in Mansion House. She and her son John supported the founding of the Andover Theological Seminary, but the family soon fell on hard times due to John Phillips' debts and subsequent bankruptcy. Phoebe Phillips was forced to sell Mansion House to the seminary's trustees, in part to pay off her pledges to the school. She resided at Farrar House until her death in 1812.

The trustees ran the mansion as a boarding house for a few years, and then turned it into a tavern and inn. Over the years, visitors included the Marquis de Lafayette, Ralph Waldo Emerson, Daniel Webster, Mark Twain, William Dean Howells, and Presidents Andrew Jackson, Martin Van Buren, and Franklin Pierce. Late one night in November 1887, an arsonist set fire to Mansion House, burning it to the ground. Only its two massive chimneys remained in the morning. After briefly considering rebuilding Mansion House, the trustees decided to move the tavern business to Stowe House, then on Chapel Avenue.

26. Brick House Site *1833; demolished*

Next door to Mansion House was a three-story brick house, its gable end toward Main Street, variously called the "printing office" and the "bookstore." Printers Timothy Flagg and Abraham Gould built it in 1833 to house their printing business, having outgrown the second floor of Mark Newman's store across the street. Newman's son Mark joined the enterprise, but soon after Flagg died and the firm was dissolved in 1841. Other printers, including Timothy Flagg's son John, ran the Brick House's press until 1854, when Warren Draper bought the building and added a bookstore on the first floor. In the 1860s Draper moved his entire business to downtown Andover. The building became a boarding house for academy students, especially those displaced when the last of the English Commons was moved off campus in 1906.

About 1908 the trustees acquired Brick House and continued to use it as a dormitory. By 1912 two new dormitories, Adams and Bishop Halls, had been built directly behind it. Brick House was in poor repair, and the living conditions of its residents were "far from satisfactory," in the words of one inside source. The expense of restoring the building to an acceptable level seemed wasteful, and in the summer of 1912, "one of the historic, but certainly unartistic landmarks of the Hill," according to *The Phillips Bulletin*, was torn down.

Across Main Street, just south of Memorial Tower, is the former residence of Mark Newman, the academy's principal from 1794 to 1809. Before he retired, Newman built this new house, as well as a store farther south on Main Street. In 1818 when Newman traded the house for an off-campus residence owned by the academy, seminary professor James Murdoch moved in. Among the academy students who boarded with him was Oliver Wendell Holmes, who lived in the northeast room on the second floor.

Under its next tenant, Professor Emerson, Newman House became a familiar stop on the Underground Railroad during the Civil War. In the twentieth century, James C. Sawyer, treasurer of Phillips Academy, lived in Newman House. Sawyer was a major ally of architect Charles Platt and alumnus Thomas Cochran, who sponsored many new buildings on campus.

Newman House is architecturally unusual. Described by one woman who grew up across the street as a "simple structure with gable roof" as late as the 1820s, the house has been altered repeatedly, though the chronology of these changes is not clear. On the north front façade, the roof was raised and the second floor extended out over two bay windows and an enclosed vestibule. Directly above, in the center of the overhang, is a Palladian window. The bay to the west of the entry was added at an even later date. An Italianate veranda was built on the south side, probably in the mid-nineteenth century, and partially enclosed in the mid-twentieth century. Original feather-edge clapboards remain on all but the north face.

Newman House

Mark Newman had a long career as a prominent businessman and community leader. His store on Main Street sold a variety of goods. The second floor housed a more significant enterprise in Academy Hill's history, a printing press. During 1812 and 1813, printers Timothy Flagg, Abraham Gould, and Jonathan Leavitt arrived in Andover to set up a press for the theological seminary, fresh from apprenticeships in Cambridge. Flagg and Gould were printers, Leavitt a binder. Together they published theological and educational volumes out of Newman's store. It was there in 1813 that Moses Stuart printed his Hebrew grammar, the first Hebrew-language book published in America. The temperance newspaper, *The Journal of Humanity*, was published for many years on the second floor of Newman House. The business prospered and when it had outgrown the space in 1833, Flagg and Gould moved to the brick building across the street. Newman's store was used by a variety of proprietors until 1897, when it was demolished.

28. Moses Stuart House   *1810–1812*

At the southern end of Faculty Row is the unpretentious Federal style house built by William Bartlet for Moses Stuart, Professor of Sacred Literature. Stuart's daughter, Sarah Stuart Robbins, reminisced about her childhood home in her autobiographical *Old Andover Days*:

> Mr. Bartlett [sic] had bought for the Seminary the six acres of land on which it was to stand, and had given my father carte blanche to 'build a dwelling house thereon according to his pleasure.' The house, though perfectly simple, was large and commodious. Behind and about it were the barns, sheds, and storerooms made necessary by the conditions of existence in those primitive time. . . . We had to keep our own cow, and our own hens. We had to raise and store many of our supplies. We depended besides upon our own horse and carriage. All this necessitated, even for a professor in a theological seminary, a certain amount of stock, implements, and service; and it called for an array of outbuildings which have since fallen into disuse and have been torn down. When the establishment was finished, and Mr. Bartlett came to inspect it, he said in his simple, brief manner,—'This is exactly such a house as a professor ought to have.'

Clearly Mr. Bartlet and Professor Stuart saw eye-to-eye more than did Bartlet and Edward Dorr Griffin.

The original Federal-style residence has been altered several times, thus blurring the chronology of its development. The main section has two entrances, suggesting it either was built in two stages or that it was con-

Moses Stuart House

structed to house more than Professor Stuart and his family, which seems unlikely. Both sections have Federal-era feather-edge clapboards, window trim, and interior moldings. The quarter round fans in the east gable end are original and the door on the western half of the main house is derived from an illustration in Asher Benjamin's *The Country Builder's Assistant* (1797). The eastern half of the house underwent a major renovation in the late nineteenth century. This may have occurred before the south wing was added in 1893. By 1909 Sarah Robbins remarked, "the various changes and additions, with the removal of the outbuildings, have made the present structure almost unrecognizable."

Indeed, one of Sarah Robbins' personal legacies was a rather dramatic change she made, which must have surprised a good many people on Andover Hill, including her parents. In the 1830s, when all of Faculty Row was painted white, Sarah and a sister saw a fashionable house in Newburyport painted a dull shade of tan, called "drab" at the time. The girls found a sample of the color and without conferring with their parents, had their house painted in "the worldly shade." Sarah Stuart remembered, "My father only looked at us and drew his red silk handkerchief across his mouth."

Moses Stuart lived in this house until his death in 1854. At the turn of the century it was occupied by Professor George Harris, who later became President of Amherst College. The south wing was added for him in 1893. One hundred years later Moses Stuart House is still used a faculty residence.

Blanchard House

29. Blanchard House   *circa 1789*

Past Moses Stuart House, Hidden Field Road takes a sharp left around the West Quad dormitories and in front of Blanchard House. Blanchard was built on Salem Street, opposite Hardy House, and by 1789 John Blanchard was licensed to board academy boys there. Blanchard's nephew Amos lived with his uncle while he attended Phillips Academy in 1787 and 1788. Amos later worked as an assistant to Samuel Farrar, and negotiated the sale of the first academy in 1802. In 1804 he created what was probably the first map of the academy grounds. Amos Blanchard was a trusted colleague of Samuel Phillips, Mark Newman, Samuel Farrar, and many of the seminary professors. Active in the local community, he was one of the founding directors of Abbot Academy in 1828.

By 1812 Phoebe Foxcroft Phillips owned Blanchard House. (Amos Blanchard built a new residence on Main Street.) Together with all her property, she sold it in 1812 to the trustees, who in turn rented it to Josiah Clough, the typesetter at Flagg and Gould's printing shop. Clough's daughter Elizabeth boarded academy students at Blanchard for many years. In 1858, Blanchard House was moved about one hundred yards east on Salem Street, and in 1928, it was moved again, to Hidden Field Road, this time to make way for Commons.

Blanchard House is important for its age and long history of association with Phillips Academy. Its most distinctive architectural feature is the west entry vestibule, a fine example of Greek revival design. It probably dates from the 1840s, although it may have been added in 1858, when the house was moved to its second location on Salem Street and reoriented with the gable end facing the street. Original eighteenth-century features remain: narrow wooden clapboards, a raking cornice on the gable ends, and pedimented dormers with multi-pane sash.

30. Jewett-Tucker House *Merrill & Eaton, 1880*

Next to Blanchard House stands Jewett-Tucker House, an exuberant Queen Anne style gem. Although moved from Main Street and remodeled for a dormitory, the exterior of Jewett-Tucker has changed very little. The variety of surface treatments, including clapboards and shingles, the steeply pitched roof with wide over-hanging eaves, and a balustrade at the peak are original features that authenticate this Queen Anne house. The windows and porches, with their heavy turned posts and balusters, are original. Recent repainting in a polychrome scheme has brought out all of Jewett-Tucker's extraordinary decorative details.

Both Otis Merrill and John Eaton did other work in Andover. Eaton had designed the public library, Memorial Hall, in 1873; Merrill, with his then partner, Arthur Cutler, designed Graves Hall in 1882 and two years later, Phillips Hall for the academy. [see Walk Three]

For the building of this house, the Reverend William R. Jewett, offered the trustees $6,000, an inducement to bring his adopted son, William Jewett Tucker, to Andover as Bartlet Professor of Sacred Rhetoric. The trustees and Tucker accepted the arrangement. Even given this stylish house, Professor Tucker remained only a short time in Andover before moving on to Dartmouth College.

Jewett–Tucker House

Commonly known as simply Tucker, the house was moved from the corner of Main and Phillips Streets in 1929 to its present location. By then considered an architectural monstrosity, it disrupted the Vista from Samuel Phillips Hall. Like its former neighbor Churchill House, it is now appraised as an outstanding example of early Queen Anne architecture.

31. Thompson House   *Edwin R. Clark, 1919*

Hidden Field Road turns sharply left at Tucker House, leading to a brick Georgian revival style dwelling, Thompson House. Charles D. Thompson, an executive of the Merrimac Paper Company in Lawrence, built this residence in 1919. At the time he had no connection to Phillips Academy. (His son was a 1938 graduate.) There is no record of just why Phillips permitted Thompson to build on this lot between Moorehead House and the West Quad dormitories. Presumably, the trustees planned to sell off various lots to private citizens while controlling the property. James Sawyer, the academy treasurer, was involved, as was the academy's landscape architect, Olmsted Brothers, who reviewed the siting of the house on the lot. In any case, Phillips purchased Thompson House in 1959 and it has been a faculty residence ever since.

Built fifteen years after Moorehead House next door, this residence was designed in style and materials more in keeping with the West Quad dorms. Thompson may have been intended to be the first of several brick single-family dwellings in this area. It is a fairly conventional interpretation of the Georgian revival style.

Thompson House

Moorehead House

32. Moorehead House   *Guy Lowell, 1904*

Warren K. Moorehead headed the archaeology department at Phillips, and
was well known for his fieldwork in New England. Lowell built Moorehead's
residence on academy land, two years after completing the Peabody
Museum on Main Street. It was the first single-family residence erected on
Hidden Field Road, which emerged piecemeal as a concentrated neighborhood of faculty housing.

Designed in the Italian Renaissance revival manner that Lowell
favored at the time, the house is typical of the architect's small domestic
work. It incorporates motifs derived from Italian villa architecture: the low-
pitched hipped roof, wide over-hanging eaves, and an emphasis on horizon-
tal lines. Double hung sash with multi-pane lights are arranged singly or in
groups of three. The original portico with columns, piers, and cornice is
trimmed with a re-created balustrade.

33. Hidden Field Road Houses *Perry, Shaw, & Hepburn, 1937*

Greenough House

Quincy House

The five houses at the end of Hidden Field Road form a neighborhood unit, a suburban cul-de-sac of modest homes designed by Perry, Shaw, & Hepburn. They are the result of a long campaign by the school to build houses for the faculty. In 1936 the Olmsted Brothers designed an elaborate "village" of 18 houses organized around a green. Finances did not allow the school to move forward at the time. In 1938 Edward Harkness donated the funds for construction of only five houses.

Each house is different and yet, as variations on the colonial revival theme, the five are clearly related. Each house shows very careful attention to detailing employed to capture the spirit of eighteenth-century architecture, rather than replicating it. Greenough House, for example, has dormers and windows that would not have been used on a house of this type. Yet its clapboard siding, large central chimney, and paneled front door with pilasters and transom are all charming colonial details.

Palmer House

Lowell House

At Quincy House Perry, Shaw, & Hepburn attached a gambrel roof ell to a gable roof house, a combination unheard of in the eighteenth century. The stylized fan over the front door is also a colonial revival feature. Similarly, Palmer House has two different types of dormers and a side ell that would not have been built two hundred years earlier. The circular lattice portico at Lowell House is a colonial revival device, as are the fan and swags on the doorway. Finally, the windows in the main body of Lowell House are unlike any made in the eighteenth century. As a group, the Hidden Field Road houses represent Perry, Shaw, & Hepburn at the peak of its creative output. At the time, the architects had acquired a national reputation for their work at Colonial Williamsburg.

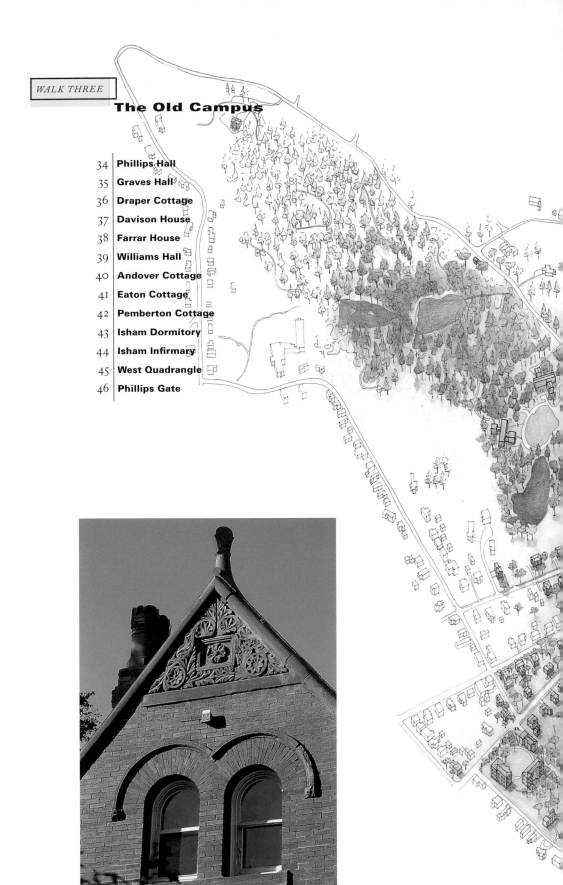

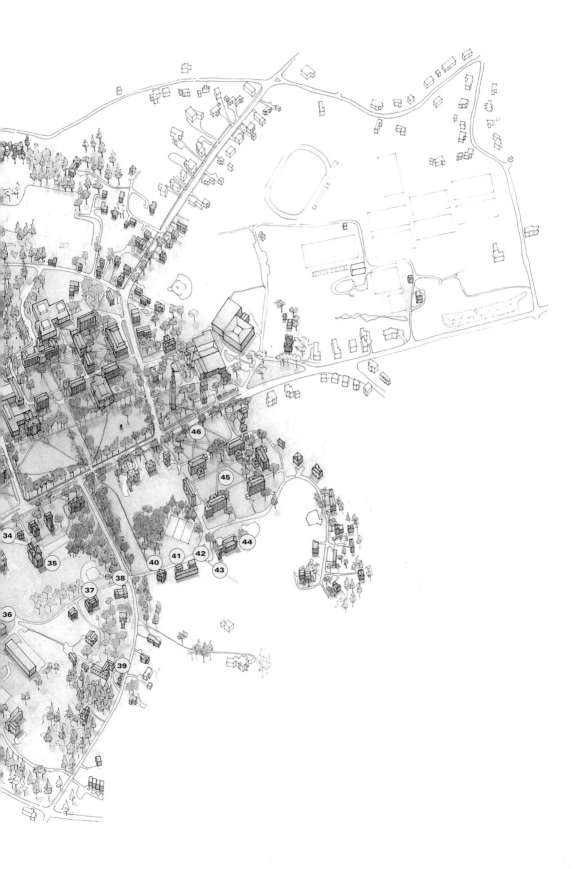

West of Main Street

In the decades following the Civil War, Phillips Academy made its first concerted effort to create a distinct campus, separate from the more prominent Andover Theological Seminary. The property behind Faculty Row was part of the original acreage purchased by the academy in 1778 and it had remained largely undeveloped. When the Stone Academy burned in December 1864, the trustees decided very quickly to establish a new, centralized campus for Phillips on the west side of Main Street. Over the next 60 years they erected buildings for classrooms, offices, and dormitories. Much of what was planned for the west side during those years was not realized, but it was part of a vigorous debate that ultimately determined the face of the Phillips Academy campus today.

With the loss of the Stone Academy, the immediate need in January 1865 was for a new main Academy, a single building that would house classrooms, a chapel, and an assembly hall. Within weeks of the fire, the trustees chose the site at the intersection of Main and School Streets (about where Samaritan House now stands). By June they had hired as their architect Charles A. Cummings. The academy went up very quickly and was dedicated in February 1866. Graves Hall, a science building, followed, and then Phillips Hall, for administrative offices. The land behind Graves, defined by the rows of English Commons on the north and Latin Commons on the south at Phillips Street, was graded for playing fields.

Main Academy, 1872

Latin Commons, circa 1886

By 1885 the trustees had created a core campus for the academy. While most students still lived in scattered locations, including Brick House on Main Street and at the run-down Latin and English Commons, and ate their meals at Major Marland's (now Clement House), and other "boarding" houses, the academic and administrative functions were now, for the first time, firmly clustered together.

The need to provide on-campus housing for all academy boys was of concern to school officials, particularly Cecil Bancroft, who was principal from 1873 to 1901. Bancroft had in mind a self-contained community for his boys, where parents could trust that even their younger sons would be well supervised. He conceived a plan for a series of small cottages, each housing a dozen boys and a resident faculty member. These cottages, he reasoned, would be small enough to allow good supervision and create a sense of community, so crucial to morale in an academic setting.

The boys, in fact, had taken this matter of *esprit de corps* into their own hands when they created secret societies, social fraternities or clubs, to which they could belong. Although they could neither eat nor live in the society clubhouses, the boys clung loyally to their societies, refusing to give them up, even when so ordered by the school. Eventually and painfully, the societies were phased out and the buildings purchased by the academy. They still furnish some of the most charming architecture on campus.

During Bancroft's tenure, the trustees hired Frederick Law Olmsted's prestigious firm to provide a master plan for the academy campus on the west side of Main Street. The 1891 design shows a string of proposed

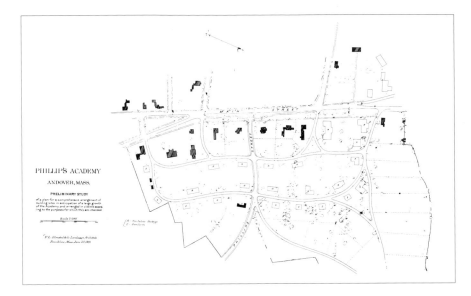

F. L. Olmsted & Co. plan for west side of Main Street, 1891

residential and classroom buildings on two new roads that looped from School Street, behind the main buildings and Faculty Row, and across Phillips Street all the way to Main Street. The academy erected three small cottages and a larger dormitory on what is now called Old Campus Road; a fourth cottage filled in a gap left by a fire in the row of English Commons. Although the need for a single dining hall was clear, and the school even went as far as the solicitation of revised plans from at least two architectural firms, no action was taken, presumably due to lack of funds.

Following Bancroft's sudden death in 1901, headmaster Alfred Stearns took up many of his predecessor's causes. The housing shortage was eased somewhat by ebbing enrollment at the seminary, which had extra space available. With only ten seminarians registered in 1902, the trustees were willing to rent Bartlet Hall to the academy as a dormitory. Stearns could finally begin to demolish or sell off the decrepit old Latin and English Commons. Once Borden Gym came on line in 1902, Bulfinch Hall was remodeled as a dining hall. Just when it seemed the academy had finally achieved a physical plant sufficient to its needs, the main Academy was declared structurally unsafe. Although repairs were made almost immediately, no renovation would transform the old Victorian era building into a modern facility.

Once again, the trustees engaged the Olmsteds to refine their master plan to answer their present and future needs: a replacement main building, an infirmary, one or two new classroom buildings, a library, and a system of large dormitories that would be more economical to build and maintain than Bancroft-style cottages. The Olmsted Brothers' 1903 solution was far different from the picturesque, park-like campus of 1891. This time the plan was more formal, organized around quadrangles rather than mean-

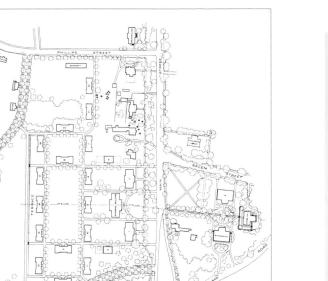

Olmsted Brothers, Phillips Academy Preliminary Plan, 1903

dering roads, with all future construction concentrated south of Phillips Street, essentially abandoning the "Old Main" campus.

In the meantime, the trustees were discussing the ultimate disposition of the Andover Theological Seminary. Enrollment and finances had declined to a point of no return, but the trustees were reluctant to make the decision to close or move the seminary. Either way, the academy was the obvious beneficiary of its property. When the seminary did leave Andover, the administration and alumni scrambled to raise the funds necessary to purchase the property, but had no clear idea what to do with it.

The "west-siders" among the trustees remained committed to the Olmsteds' plan of 1903. Even with the acquisition of Bartlet and Foxcroft, the academy still required more dormitory space. A flurry of architectural activity between 1911 and 1913 produced four new dorms and an infirmary, all designed by Guy Lowell. Day Hall was built in line with Seminary Row on the east side. Three more dormitories, similar in scale, joined Bancroft Hall to form three sides of a new quadrangle set back from Main Street on the west side, in compliance with the Olmsteds' scheme. Lowell's Isham Infirmary was completed nearby.

The $200,000 price tag for the seminary property put a severe strain on the academy's resources, and no commitments for new construction were made. In the early 1910s, the alumni played a major role in eliminating the debt, and in the process gained a foothold in the power structure of the trustees. This power shift would have profound impact on campus development in the 1920s.

Guy Lowell, Proposed Master Plan for Campus West of Main Street, 1919

After a hiatus during World War I, attention again turned to a new main academy. In January 1919 Guy Lowell designed an ambitious Memorial Auditorium in honor of Phillips Academy graduates who had died in the war. Although the Olmsted Brothers recommended two sites for it on the east side of Main Street, the trustees remained steadfastly attached to the west side. Within months, Lowell expanded his plan to encompass an auditorium, administrative offices, and classrooms in a huge new academy headquarters on axis with Bulfinch Hall. The dormitories built between 1911 and 1913 would serve as a kind of forecourt, with a freestanding Memorial Tower at the center.

Academy alumni, particularly the major fundraisers who had just retired the seminary property debt, began to assert pressure to consider other sites. George Case, P.A. 1890, pointed out that the topography, which ran downhill, was inappropriate for a memorial monument. Others suggested the site directly across from Seminary Row, where the Vista now extends west. Lowell rejected that site as too isolated. Case countered with the ridge behind Seminary Row. As other powerful alumni began joining the debate, the trustees diplomatically offered to hire a consulting architect. Their choice in June 1921 was Charles A. Platt of New York City. In short order, Platt reviewed the Olmsteds' 1903 plan and chose instead the site behind Pearson Hall for the new main Academy building. Within a year, a new master plan was completed, shifting the future of Phillips Academy irrevocably to the east side of campus, and binding it with the oldest part of the theological seminary.

Today, the Old Campus is almost entirely residential. Cummings' old Main Academy was repeatedly renovated and finally demolished in 1927. Graves Hall is now devoted to the Music Department and diminutive

Phillips Hall houses the academy's Public Safety offices. The original Isham Infirmary became a dormitory when a modern wing provided more up-to-date medical facilities. Cecil Bancroft's cottages on Old Campus Road remain popular small dormitories, and the former principal would be gratified by the fact that with the completion of the west quadrangle of dorms in the 1930s, all Phillips Academy boarding students could be housed on campus.

The Old Campus Walk begins on the west side of Main Street, opposite Chapel Avenue, with two of the three original buildings that formed the post-Civil War academy, Phillips Hall and behind it, Graves Hall.

34. Phillips Hall   *Merrill & Cutler, 1884–1885*

This Richardsonian Romanesque style office building is a handsomely detailed structure that has been remarkably well preserved and is the most important surviving Victorian structure on campus. The exterior has been altered very little, except for some repointing. The architects made the most of a small building by manipulating the massing into three distinct segments, embellished with quarry-faced sandstone and terra cotta panels, planted firmly on a granite base. The interior also retains many original finishes. The woodwork, including wainscoting and floors throughout the building, has survived intact. Two masonry fireplace surrounds, one in each of the first floor rooms, are characteristic of late nineteenth-century design.

Principal Cecil Bancroft in his Phillips Hall office, 1896

Phillips Hall

Phillips Hall was the first administration building on campus. It housed an office for the principal, where the trustees met, and the treasurer's office adjacent to a walk-in vault. The building was donated by the current treasurer, Edward Taylor, who wrote to the trustees upon its completion,

> I desire to give expression to the gratitude I feel, for so long a term of service, as your Treasurer, as well as of satisfaction, that I have been permitted to see the erection of a tasteful, convenient, and substantial building for the use of the Principal of the Academy, and the Treasurer.

Taylor had reason to be grateful. His former office, a primitive wooden building, was relegated to use as an athletic field house.

After the administrative offices moved across Main Street to Brechin Hall in 1910, this building was used as the Phillips Club, a faculty retreat where teachers could relax over cards, coffee, and cigarettes. (The faculty was not allowed to smoke in public.) Phillips Hall is now the headquarters of Public Safety.

Phillips Hall was designed by prominent Lowell architectural firm of Merrill & Cutler, whose junior partner, Arthur S. Cutler, was an Andover native. Otis Merrill and his former associate, John Eaton, had designed Tucker House four years earlier.

35. Graves Hall *Merrill & Cutler, 1882–1883; 1891–1892*

In 1882 Merrill & Cutler prepared designs for Graves Hall on a site well back from Main Street. The original plans for a chemical laboratory and classrooms had to be modified, presumably for financial reasons, and the building was constructed in two stages. The east wing, with its narrow end toward School Street, housed the laboratory, and was finished in 1883. Nine years later, the much larger western section provided the classroom space sorely needed by the Science Department.

Architectural taste had changed in the intervening years, a change reflected in the shift from Queen Anne to Romanesque elements. The dominant feature here is the main entrance, which appears to be the base of a tower without the shaft. The doors are recessed behind a great round arch at the top of a flight of stairs. Above the arch is an open porch with a stone balustrade.

Graves was sited directly south of Charles Cummings's Main Academy, built nearly thirty years before. Connected by footpaths, these two buildings were the core of the new Phillips Academy campus. With the demolition of the Academy in 1927, Graves Hall lost its orientation. The entrance tower still indicates the primary façade, but it now faces a nondescript lot, overgrown with shrubbery.

Graves Hall

Draper Cottage

36. Draper Cottage *attributed to Alexander Wadsworth Longfellow, 1892–1893*

Southwest of Graves Hall, lies Draper Cottage, the last of Cecil Bancroft's four small dormitories. Draper replaced one of the wooden English Commons, which had burned down, leaving a gap in the row of six identical buildings. The academy was anxious to replace the decrepit old Commons as soon as possible and, according to the Olmsted 1891 plan, additional dormitories were to take their place.

Draper Cottage closely resembled Longfellow's Pemberton Cottage built the preceding year. An April 1892 letter from Longfellow to Alpheus Hardy, treasurer of the board of trustees, suggested that his firm was willing to allow the academy to duplicate his plan for Pemberton Cottage for a token fee. "In regard to putting up other buildings from these same drawings, we have talked it over, and we think that $50. for each building would be a fair charge for the use of the designs. . . ." Six months later, *The Phillipian*, the academy newspaper, announced, "The Draper Cottage, now being built on the site of the old second house, English Commons, will be exactly like [Pemberton] and will be ready for occupancy in January." This cottage was funded by Warren Draper, the printer who began his career at Brick House on Main Street in 1854, and was by 1893 a very prosperous merchant.

Three stories tall, Draper Cottage was designed for ten students and a faculty member. Many of its original features are still intact, including the main entrance and pedimented portico supported on columns. The hipped roof, double-hung sash with multi-pane lights, and cornice with modillions and dentils are all characteristic colonial revival details. The side entrance and its portico are not original. Regrettably, the interior was entirely gutted in 1989 and no historic fabric survives. Draper Hall remains a dormitory.

37. Davison House   *Perry, Shaw & Hepburn, 1928*

Old Campus Road continues west and south around the athletic fields behind Graves to Tilton House, a textbook Georgian revival brick house designed by Guy Lowell's successor firm, Henry & Richmond, for a secret society. Next is Davison House, the first Perry, Shaw & Hepburn commission for Phillips Academy, completed before the firm gained a national reputation for their work at Colonial Williamsburg. The use of the Tudor style reflects the eclectic character of their earlier work, before they became so closely associated with the colonial revival.

Constructed in 1928 for the secret society Phi Lamda Delta or FLD, Davison House has been beautifully preserved. Using little decorative trim, the architects relied on elegantly detailed materials to convey a sense of quality and sophistication. Brick walls laid in an English bond, ashlar masonry trim, and a slate roof with copper gutters and downspouts are typical of the vernacular tradition emulated by the Tudor revival.

The intersection of Old Campus Road and Phillips Street is the site of the George Abbot House, in which Samuel Phillips Jr. lived with his family when Phillips Academy was founded. Subsequently, the house was occupied by the first three preceptors of the academy, Eliphalet Pearson, Ebenezer Pemberton, and Mark Newman. Leonard Woods, Professor of Sacred Literature at the seminary, lived here for nine years until his own home, Pease House, was built in 1817. The old house then became a dining commons, called the Shawsheen Club by academy boys, and gradually deteriorated. By 1889 it had to be demolished.

Davison House

Farrar House

38. Farrar House *1811–1812*

Farrar House stands just west of the old Abbot house site. Built by Samuel Farrar, treasurer of the board of trustees from 1809 to 1840, the house was moved from its original location on Main Street to this site on Phillips Street in 1881. Like several of the Federal-era houses on Faculty Row, it is typical of the homes built by prosperous merchants in Salem and Newburyport. Used for many years as a boarding house and then a dormitory, Farrar is now a faculty residence.

Farrar has undergone significant changes over the years. The front portico and west porch are colonial revival additions. Although the clapboards, cornice, and window trim are also not original, they replicate early-nineteenth-century features. An unusual survivor is the extended farmhouse plan consisting of a long ell between the house and the carriage barn. In 1881, Phillips Street was still very much a rural location.

Farther west on Phillips Street, past Hayward House, is the large colonial revival building affectionately called "Will Hall." Until the spring of 1999, Will Hall was a dormitory. It is currently leased to the town of Andover as a potential Senior Center, and is not open to the public.

In 1890 Amos Blanchard, a member of a prominent local family who had been treasurer of the Boston & Maine Railroad for forty years, built a new residence in Andover, still visible as the center section of Will Hall. Edward H. Williams Jr. purchased the house in 1901 and hired the Boston architect James T. Kelley to design additions and alterations costing $30,000. Kelley substantially enlarged the building into a gentleman's farm estate

Nine years later, Williams sold the house to Phillips Academy, well below its market value. The academy was actively trying to attract younger boys, 13- and 14-year-olds, whose families were unwilling to send their sons to poorly supervised boarding houses. Williams Hall was the perfect solution. It was immediately converted to a dorm for "juniors," the youngest boys on campus. By 1999 it was no longer needed by the academy and an alternate use was sought to avoid demolition. Similar to the old laundry on the Abbot campus, which is now a day care center [see Walk Four], the building was made available for community use.

Many of the original features of the H-shaped building have survived. The main entrance with portico, sidelights, and transom, and the second-story door above, framed with pilasters and broken scroll pediment are

Williams Hall

intact. Wooden clapboards, quoins, and cornice are original, as are the double-hung windows with blinds and Palladian windows. Will Hall remains an excellent example of the large wooden colonial revival style mansions built at the end of the nineteenth century.

Back on Old Campus Road, heading south, are three of Cecil Bancroft's small cottages. Each was designed to house a dozen students and a faculty member in some combination of double and single suites, and single rooms. A double suite consisted of a common sitting room-study with two small bedrooms. Rooms were not inexpensive. For the academic year 1900–1901, for example, each boy paid the high price of $100 for a double in Andover Cottage, heat and "service" included. Bathroom facilities were in the basement. All four cottages were constructed of brick, yet smoking was banned from the beginning; the threat of fire had proven all too real on campus.

40. Andover Cottage *George W. Cole, 1892*

Andover Cottage, as the name implies, has local associations that are not strictly connected to the academy or the seminary. This was the first planned dormitory (although it was completed after Pemberton) and the idea caught the attention of townspeople. A kind of spontaneous fund-raising campaign began, spearheaded by Miss Emily Carter, who ran a boarding house for academy boys, to collect the $9,000 to construct the cottage. At a citizens' committee meeting about the new cottage in May 1891, John Phelps Taylor, representing the academy, made an unabashed plea for financial support. The more reserved headmaster Cecil Bancroft did not attend, but sent a letter to be read aloud to the crowd. It said in part,

> The erection of an Andover Cottage will be the beginning of a movement which will continue till both rows of our dormitories [the old Latin and English Commons] are replaced by buildings more suitable for their purpose, more worthy of the fame of the Academy and an ornament to the town. The Andover Cottage will be a thing complete in itself, and the promise of better things to come.

Miss Carter raised over $5,300 that evening.

Andoverites seemed pleased with the building when they showed up for the public open house in January 1893. The local paper reported,

> The result of the examination seemed to be one of apparent satisfaction. It is certainly a well planned and a most comfortable building. One could not ask for better quarters. . . . The building is every way a credit to architect, builder, Academy and to the citizens of Andover.

Andover Cottage

The effort no doubt benefited from the selection of architect George W. Cole, the son and nephew of prominent local businessmen. Cole had trained in Boston in the office of Shepley, Rutan, & Coolidge and had been sent to New London, Connecticut, to supervise a job. He settled there permanently, but maintained a partnership with Joseph E. Chandler in Boston. Six months after Andover Cottage opened, Cole died suddenly at the age of 27. On his own, Chandler became perhaps the leading expert on American colonial architecture in New England.

Surprisingly, Andover Cottage's design was inspired by Tudor references, not colonial, like the other three cottages. Cole & Chandler were emulating Oxford and Eton Colleges, although as Chandler admitted in an 1892 letter to John Olmsted, "it may be hardly recognizable as such because of our forced economy in architectural detail." Cecil Bancroft had traveled in England in 1878 visiting Eton, Harrow, Rugby, and other schools. He was impressed with their educational systems, their campus facilities, and, of course, the sense of history and tradition evident in their buildings. There seems to have been considerable confusion among the architect, landscape architect, and the academy over the siting of the cottage and its style as late as March 1892. At that point Chandler stated that it was too late to switch to a colonial revival design without additional costs. In any case, its unique appearance seems to have made it more popular in the end. The *Andover Townsman* reported that many visitors liked it best. "Its architecture is more pleasing than that of the other cottages and its rooms are considered the most attractive."

The key architectural feature of Andover Cottage is clearly the romantic central pavilion, with its crenallated second-story porch and lancet-arched entrance. Windows are grouped in twos and threes, and the roof has multiple gable ends. Two corbelled chimneys have been lost and the door is a contemporary replacement. Unfortunately, the interior of Andover, like all the 1890s cottages, was completely gutted in 1987. No historic fabric survived.

41. Eaton Cottage   *George C. Harding, 1892–1893*

Next to Andover is Eaton Cottage, originally called Bancroft in honor of the principal who had pushed for the construction of the new dorms. Unlike Andover Cottage, Eaton was designed in the colonial revival style, with a gambrel roof covered in slate and double-hung sash with multi-pane lights set in a symmetrical arrangement around a square portico.

Its architect, George C. Harding, was just starting out in his practice when he received the commission from the academy. He graduated from the MIT School of Architecture in 1889 and was working as a draughtsman. Sometime in 1892 he moved to Pittsfield, Massachusetts, where he established a very successful career. Harding was a most conscientious architect. During the summer of 1894, he wrote Cecil Bancroft asking approval to replace the furring and lath around the chimneys at Eaton College with fireproof wire lath, at his own expense. Although reassured by experts, including an MIT professor, that the existing construction met current standards and was adequate, Harding wrote, "Nevertheless I am not satisfied to have any but the best & safest construction in any building I am responsible for."

Bancroft was renamed Eaton Cottage in 1901 after the larger Bancroft Hall dormitory was dedicated. James S. Eaton, a former English teacher who also taught math, philosophy, and bookkeeping, resided at the academy almost twenty years, 1847 to 1865.

Eaton Cottage

South of Eaton is Pemberton Cottage, which was originally called Taylor Cottage and sited on Phillips Street, just west of Old Campus Road, in com-pliance with Olmsted's 1891 master plan. In 1928 it was moved to its cur-rent location because it interfered with Charles Platt's Vista. Like Eaton, Taylor Cottage was renamed after a larger dormitory was dedicated in honor of its namesake. John Phelps Taylor was a professor at the seminary who had lobbied tirelessly for financial support for the cottage dormitories. In 1913, one of Guy Lowell's new West Quad

Pemberton Cottage

dormitories was called Taylor Hall [see below] and the cottage was renamed Pemberton, after the preceptor of Phillips Academy from 1786 to 1793.

The trustees chose Alexander Wadsworth Longfellow of the presti-gious Boston architectural firm, Longfellow, Alden & Harlow, for this, the first cottage dormitory. A nephew of the famous poet, Longfellow was one of the earliest proponents of the colonial revival style. He later designed several dormitories at Harvard.

Longfellow's design for Pemberton Cottage is an elegant attempt to freely interpret early American architectural motifs. A three-story building with a symmetrical front façade and hipped roof, it is a diminutive distant cousin of Federal-era houses such as Farrar House, constructed in brick. The front portico with sidelights, with a Palladian window and balustrade above, is also related to Federal prototypes, but in somewhat awkward new pro-portions. Single double-hung wooden windows with shutters flank the cen-tral element on the first two stories, then suddenly multiply to five shorter windows on the third floor. Pemberton drew mixed reviews when it opened in the fall of 1892, especially when compared to Andover Cottage. It was described in local newspapers as, "rather plain in appearance."

43. Isham Dormitory *Guy Lowell, 1913*

Just past the row of cottages is the building Guy Lowell designed as an infirmary. At the time of its construction this was an isolated and quiet spot. Isham is now used as a dormitory. Doctors at Massachusetts General Hospital advised Phillips on the layout and equipment; according to publicity in 1912 the infirmary was more up to date than medical facilities at any other private school. Isham Infirmary had its own kitchen and service staff, isolation wards for contagious disease, an operating room, even rooms for parents of ailing children. Sunshine and fresh air were considered important aids to recovery, so Lowell designed sleeping porches on either end and sited the building facing north so that the wards in the east and west wings would get as much sunlight as possible.

On the exterior, Isham appears to be a large and elegant mansion, intentionally more home-like than institutional, so as to not intimidate academy boys who needed medical attention. This was the eighth building Lowell designed for Phillips, and he was comfortable in his role and with the colonial revival style. He chose his favorite Georgian features: a central pavilion and entrance portico, a Palladian window above, and double-hung sash windows with multi-pane lights. The refined domestic character of the building is, however, almost overwhelmed by the four massive pairs of brick chimneys that rise from the gambrel roof. The symmetrical sleeping porches were originally open at ground level, and did not extend the rectangular mass of the building. The end porches reinforce the symmetry of the building and enhance its gracious scale.

Isham Dormitory

Isham Infirmary

44. Isham Infirmary   *Perry, Shaw, & Hepburn, 1934*

The design of early-twentieth-century medical facilities changed rapidly and by 1928, Isham Infirmary was obsolete and too small to accommodate the growing academy population. Although the trustees considered building an entirely new structure that Charles Platt designed for them, in the end they opted to add a large wing on the south side of Lowell's infirmary. They hired Perry, Shaw, & Hepburn, a prestigious Boston firm, to design the new wing. With this commission the architects replaced the recently deceased Platt as the official architects of Phillips Academy.

Designed to be compatible with Lowell's building, the addition extends from the center of the south façade, creating a T-shaped building. Lowell's paired chimneys and hipped roof are repeated, with the addition of a roof monitor. A two-story sleeping porch-solarium at the south end echoes those on the older building. Perry, Shaw, & Hepburn replaced Lowell's supporting columns, heavy decorative cornice, and Chinese Chippendale style balustrade, with simpler overall lines and an English Regency style wrought-iron railing as the one embellishment on the walls of windows.

Improved medical facilities included an in-house laboratory, updated emergency operating room, and an x-ray room. Isham Infirmary was granted hospital status in 1959. In 1978 it was renovated again with a new, accessible entrance and upgraded equipment. Lowell's original building was also remodeled at this time to serve as a dormitory.

Adams Hall

45. West Quadrangle:

Bishop Hall   *Guy Lowell, 1911*
Adams Hall   *Guy Lowell, 1912*
Taylor Hall   *Guy Lowell, 1913*
Johnson Hall   *Guy Lowell 1922*
Bancroft Hall   *Longfellow, Alden, & Harlow, 1899–1900*
Rockwell House   *Perry, Shaw, & Hepburn, 1934–1935*

The West Quadrangle is directly east of Isham, accessed on this tour by following the road around the tennis court on Old Campus Road, through a small parking lot, and entering the Quad at the northwest corner, between Bancroft Hall and Rockwell House.

West Quad is on the site of the 1903 plan by Guy Lowell and Olmsted Brothers for the central academy complex to be built on axis with Bulfinch Hall, and still contains vestiges of that plan. On the east side of the Quad are Bishop and Adams Halls. They were originally intended to flank a new central Academy set slightly to the northwest. In 1913 Taylor Hall was erected southwest of and at right angles to Adams to begin to close a quadrangle around the academy. By 1919 Lowell had expanded his plan to a much larger complex aligned with Salem Street instead of Bulfinch Hall. Bishop, Adams, and Taylor were envisioned as the northern half of a much larger

Bishop Hall

Johnson Hall

quadrangle, with an access road south of Bishop to a massive new building of classrooms, administrative offices, and an auditorium. Memorial Tower was designed as the focal point of the complex. When the school abandoned Lowell's scheme in 1921, Bishop, Adams, and Taylor were left in isolation.

Bishop Hall and Adams Hall were built as a pair of dormitories in 1911 and 1912, respectively, with their primary façades toward Main Street. Each is constructed of brick with neo-classical porticos framing entrance doors. These buildings, and the others in the Quad, reflect the standard design for a Georgian revival dormitory: a large, rectangular, three-story building with a hipped roof and multi-pane sash.

In the 1960s the west façades, facing into the quadrangle, were altered with the addition of a one-story commons room. Driveways and garages have been added on the east sides, further obscuring the orientation of the buildings and confusing the visual clues as to which is the "front" façade. Both buildings are still used as dormitories.

Taylor Hall followed in 1913, sited with its back to Hidden Field Road, facing north into the Quad. As originally designed, the building had a fairly elaborately ornamented north façade with a portico and roof balustrade. Most of these features were removed in 1965 when a commons room was added.

By the time Johnson Hall was built, directly west of Adams, Lowell knew he was planning an exclusively residential quadrangle. The memorial tower and the new main academy and administration functions were all moving to the east side of Main Street. For this less important building on a less visible site than Adams or Bishop, Lowell decided to economize on his design. Wooden door surrounds and a brick foundation substituted for more costly stone. Still, Johnson is compatible with its neighbors, with similar features, including recessed entrances with wood pilasters, entablatures, quoins, and double hung sash with multi-pane lights. The original front façade is now obscured by the 1960s commons room.

The interior of the building was divided in half, as indicated by the double entries. Each floor had more single rooms than suites, suggesting that expectations of boarding students (or their parents) had changed since the cottages were erected thirty years earlier. Privacy, more than camaraderie, seems to have been a priority in this large, comfortable dorm.

Johnson was built in 1922 in response to the impending closure of at least four local boarding houses that had accommodated academy boys. The as yet unnamed new dormitory was announced with little fanfare in the April 1922 issue of *The Phillips Bulletin:*

> Mr. Guy Lowell, of Boston, the architect, has designed a building of the Georgian Colonial type, of the same general style as the other modern dormitories and in complete harmony with the earlier structures like Phillips and Bartlet Halls. It will have rooms for forty boys, twenty on each side, with ample quarters on the first floor for two married instructors and their families.

Bancroft Hall originally stood on Phillips Street, east of Old Campus Road, not on the West Quad. Like Pemberton Cottage it was moved in 1928 to open an unobstructed view down the Vista. It was sited south of Bishop to conform to the 1903 plan to enclose the quadrangle. The Olmsted Brothers were unhappy with Bancroft Hall's original orientation, parallel to Phillips Street, and fought vigorously to have the building turned 90 degrees so that the rooms would get more sunlight. They were outvoted by the trustees and the architect.

Bancroft was the first large dormitory constructed on campus after the cottages. Designed by Alexander Wadsworth Longfellow as a more efficient housing solution, it enclosed three small-scale units into one building,

Bancroft Hall

Rockwell House

divided by firewalls; each one was to be supervised by a faculty member. Regrettably, a 1968 renovation demolished all historic interior fabric. On the exterior, Bancroft Hall is pure Georgian revival in style. The brick walls are detailed with granite door surrounds, splayed lintels, stone steps, and a base of tooled ashlar blocks. At the same time he worked on Bancroft, Longfellow was designing buildings for Harvard University and has been credited with establishing that campus's Georgian revival image.

Rockwell House was the last of the West Quad dormitories to be erected, filling in the northwest quarter. Perry, Shaw, & Hepburn were faced with the task of inserting a new building among others as much as thirty years older. Their restrained Georgian revival building is significant as a member of a coordinated ensemble, rather than a unique individual like their Davison House of 1928. Rockwell House lost both of its original long façades to 1960s additions, but the entrances on the north and south ends retain their ashlar granite door surrounds.

46. Phillips Gate   *Guy Lowell, 1914*

Between Bishop and Adams Halls and Main Street is an open lawn where Samuel Phillips Jr.'s Mansion House and the Brick House once stood. [See Walk Two] Crossed by paths, it now provides some privacy and detachment from the hubbub of local traffic for this residential area. At the Main Street sidewalk is a brick gateway, somewhat obscured by bushes. Guy Lowell designed the Phillips Gate as the formal pedestrian entry to the east side campus in 1914. It stood originally on Main Street at the foot of the path to Seminary Row. When Charles Platt transformed that pathway into the more formal Vista in 1928, Phillips Gate was relocated here on the west side.

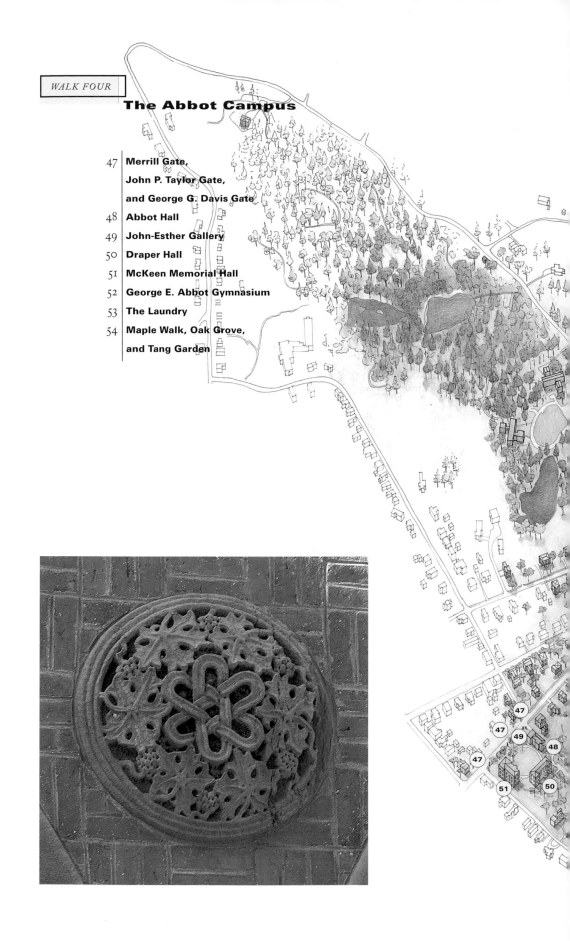

The Abbot Campus

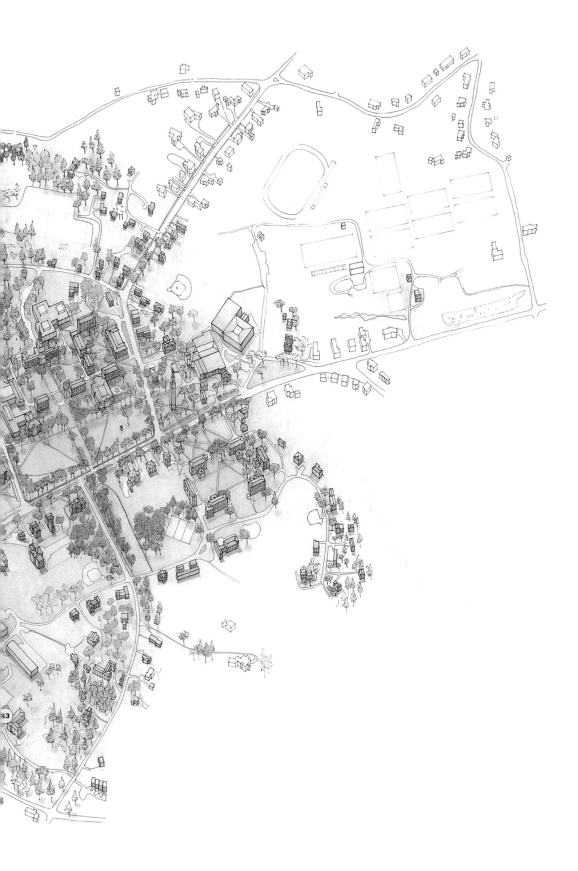

No one knows who posted handbills all around Andover in February 1828, announcing a meeting about a "female high school." We do know that some of Andover's most prominent citizens, including Samuel Farrar, treasurer of Phillips Academy, Mark Newman, principal of the academy from 1795 to 1809, local ministers, businessmen, and a state senator responded. They set to work immediately, forming committees to find a site for the proposed girls' school, determine building costs and a construction schedule, outline a fundraising plan, and draft a constitution.

They bought a lot on Main Street and erected a fence. This site caused considerable concern among the parents of prospective students, and Mrs. Moses Stuart, whose husband taught at the Andover Theological Seminary, and Mrs. John Adams, wife of the academy principal, circulated a petition requesting a change of location. The mothers objected to Main Street because the "Theologues and academy boys" frequently passed that way. (Perhaps they knew their husbands' students all too well.) Mark Newman came to the rescue, offering to donate a one-acre lot on School Street. By July, everything was in place except for funding. The trustees almost gave up in despair of ever raising enough money to build their school.

This time Samuel Farrar found the solution in the person of Mrs. Sarah Abbot, who was tied to Academy Hill by friendship, blood, and marriage. Mrs. Abbot was a close friend of the late Phoebe Foxcroft Phillips and second cousin to her husband Samuel Phillips, Jr. Her husband, Nehemiah Abbot, had been steward of the theological seminary commons. In gratitude for Sarah Abbot's $1,000 pledge, the trustees named the new academy after her. By the time her will was probated in 1850, she had given over $10,000 to Abbot Academy.

Construction began immediately and the Abbot Female Academy opened in May 1829 with seventy pupils. For a brief period, the academy was called Abbot Female Seminary, a name shortened affectionately by Phillips' boys to the "Fem Sem." The term was applied equally to the school and the students, as in "To the Fem Sems of Andover; so near and yet so far!"—a favorite toast on Academy Hill.

One of the first students recalled the early days at Abbot: "It was a great era in our lives. For years Andover had been famous for the education of boys and men, but advantages for girls must be sought elsewhere; now a handsome and convenient building had been erected." Known today as Abbot Hall, the Academy building provided only classrooms and recitation rooms. There were no boarding facilities, though girls came from all over New England to attend. At Abbot, as at Phillips Academy, students from out of town boarded in private homes, carefully selected by the trustees.

In 1856 Punchard Free School, a public high school, opened in Andover. Abbot could no longer rely on the enrollment of local girls. The

Abbot Hall after 1854

trustees felt pressure to build a suitable dormitory, but they had just managed to pay off their mortgages three years earlier. They committed to raise
$8,000 and in 1854 Smith Hall was erected just behind the Academy as
the first dormitory for Abbot girls, a large Italianate style building with
overhanging eaves and a fashionable cupola. Funds were stretched just to
cover the building. No money was left for furnishing the rooms.

Harriet Beecher Stowe, wife of seminary professor Calvin Stowe,
"threw all that glowing enthusiasm of which she is capable into a solution of
the problem," remembered one student. Mrs. Stowe planned a "festival." She

Smith Hall, circa 1885

Smith Hall dormitory room, 1885, thirty years after Harriet Beecher Stowe and her friends furnished the building

and her friends filled every room in the Academy with music, food, tea, coffee, flowers, and silver. "Never had the old 'Fem Sem' been so tastefully adorned, so brilliantly lighted, and filled with so tempting an array of good things, with such throngs of satisfied, happy people." The ladies began sewing curtains, bedding, and linens. They cajoled local merchants into discounting their goods. Three women pooled their resources to provide dinnerware. Each dormitory room was furnished "in a substantial, yet attractive manner, at the least expense," providing "bedstead, mattresses, bureau with swing glass, sink, table, chairs, towel rack, and bookcase; window-curtains and valances extra." The kitchen was modestly fitted out and other common areas—music room, dining room, and parlors—were tastefully furnished, for a total cost of $1771.

Academy Hill families were often involved at Abbot, husbands and wives, fathers and mothers serving as trustees, teachers, fundraisers, and supporters. Lectures and facilities at the Teachers' Seminary and Phillips Academy were made available to Abbot girls. Wives of teachers, like Mrs. Stowe, frequently lent a hand on special projects. The daughters of faculty and sisters of students were sent to Abbot for a rigorous education. Abbot girls quite naturally met their future husbands on Academy Hill, especially at the theological seminary, and many lived out their lives as missionaries' wives in Constantinople or Okayama, or as mistresses of American parsonages.

In 1863 the Abbot "campus" covered one acre, from School Street to just behind Smith Hall, and was tightly enclosed by a board fence. Trustee George Davis donated two additional acres west of Smith Hall, and two years later bought the house just north of the Academy. Named Davis Hall, this house became Abbot's second dormitory.

In 1859 Philena McKeen became Abbot's eleventh principal, with her sister Phebe as first assistant. Philena McKeen reigned over the "Fem Sem" for the next 33 years. Through the 1860s and 1870s, the school expanded incrementally. The academy enlarged Smith Hall with an ell and wide veranda, then in 1877 added a windmill to pump water throughout the building. Land was also purchased, and by 1878 22 acres in all had been acquired and landscaped, with Maple Walk and the Oak Grove as key features. Fifty years later an arborist with Olmsted Brothers recommended that natural development should continue, that the "splendid maple allée would stay substantially as it is." He added, the red oak grove "is about the largest and finest 'pure stand' of red oaks that we have ever encountered; it is remarkable. We cannot recall the like anywhere else. . . . We hope that future developments will allow this grove to remain intact."

For Philena McKeen the academy's late-nineteenth-century growth was too slow and she chafed at the conservative financial policies of her board of trustees. In 1878 the United States Commissioner of Education rated an Abbot education equal to that of Vassar College, Mt. Holyoke Seminary (now College), and a handful of other women's schools. Yet Miss

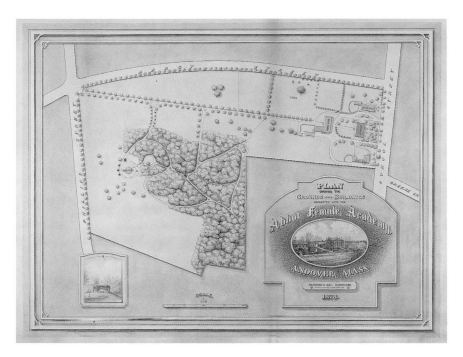

Hammond and Gay, Plan Showing the Grounds and Buildings Connected with the Abbot Female Academy, Andover, Mass., 1878

Hartwell & Richardson plan of 1886

McKeen's budget was far below those other institutions. A year earlier she discovered that the principal of Bradford Academy in Haverhill (now Bradford Junior College), was earning an annual salary of $3,000, compared to the combined salaries paid to her and her sister of $1,600. When she complained, the trustees raised the figure to $2,000.

Miss McKeen dreamed of an impressive campus, a place that showed the world that education of girls was taken seriously at Abbot Academy. In 1886 she and the trustees commissioned Hartwell & Richardson of Boston to create a master plan of her ideal campus, and launched a building campaign to raise money. Hartwell & Richardson presented an ambitious vision: a new cluster of four large Romanesque revival buildings, one for administration, chapel and recitation rooms, a large main Academy with common kitchen and dining rooms, music rooms, student and teacher hous-

Abbot, Smith, Draper, and Davis Halls, 1903

ing, and two "language halls," dormitories where only French or German would be spoken. Miss McKeen needed $150,000. She did the most of fundraising personally, but fell far short of the total. Humiliated and disappointed, she resigned from the academy. Warren Draper, however, printer, publisher, and great friend of Abbot, pledged enough to build just one

Draper Hall detail

building. He convinced Miss McKeen to withdraw her resignation. When the new hall was completed in 1890, it was named Draper Hall in his honor.

To accommodate Draper Hall, all the older buildings had to be moved. Like pawns in a giant game of chess they slowly moved around each other. The old Academy was turned 90 degrees and moved south. Smith Hall traveled west toward the Oak Grove. South Hall, ironically, moved north to Abbot Street, where it was renamed Sunset Lodge. Draper was constructed facing School Street with Davis Hall still in place on the north. A semi-circular drive, the new Abbot Circle, focused this loose quadrangle. Six years after Philena McKeen's death in 1898, the trustees replaced Davis Hall with McKeen Memorial Hall. Abbot Circle was now complete.

Merrill Gate

47. John P. Taylor Gate, Merrill Gate, and George G. Davis Gate

McKim, Mead & White, 1921

These three brick and wrought-iron gates completed the reorganization of the main buildings at Abbot by providing formal entrances to the campus. Bertha Bailey, headmistress of Abbot Academy from 1912 to 1935, had the gates closed at night and all day Sunday, sequestering the girls from what she considered the overly zealous attentions of Phillips Academy boys.

The designs date from about 1917 or 1918. By that time, both of the firm's principal designers, Charles McKim and Stanford White, had died. The individual designer of these gates has not been recorded. Nonetheless, these gates are part of a group of gateways designed by McKim, Mead & White for Harvard, Princeton, and Bowdoin College.

Abbot Hall

48. Abbot Hall   *1828–1829*

The first home of the Abbot Female Academy, Abbot Hall is an exceptional early Greek Revival building. Possibly inspired by Charles Bulfinch's Massachusetts General Hospital in Boston (1818), Abbot Hall is a very early example of what became typical of Greek revival style public and institutional buildings that arose around the country during the 1840s and 1850s. Records indicate that David Hidden of Newburyport was master builder and that William Saunders of Cambridge fabricated the Ionic columns. Both men were experienced housewrights, but it has not been established that either was responsible for the design of this structure.

Without the Ionic portico, which is very shallow and barely projects from the facade, Abbot Hall is almost Federal style in character. The masonry and wood detailing is more delicate than what came to be typical of the heavy, monumental Greek revival style. This is part of the charm of the building, for there were relatively few schools of any size in New England in 1828 with a temple front. If used at all at that time, a classical portico was more likely to have been on a bank or state house. Schools tended to look like large houses on the outside. As in many aspects of its approach, Abbot Academy was exceptionally forward thinking in its architecture. Writing about Abbot Hall in 1879, Abbie Sawyer Davis commented, "When it was ready for occupancy in 1829, it was considered a very elegant building."

John-Esther Gallery

49. John-Esther Gallery   *Andrews, Jaques, & Rantoul, 1906–1907*

In 1907 the Boston firm Andrews, Jaques, & Rantoul added a museum to the east end of Abbot Hall to house an art collection donated by Mrs. Esther Byers as well as studios. Since its inception, Abbot had offered drawing and painting classes. John-Esther Gallery only confirmed the academy's reputation for cultural education, 25 years before a similar institution—the Addison Gallery of American Art—was founded at Phillips Academy.

John-Esther Gallery detail

The School Street entrance is framed by stone columns that support a pediment with urns, limestone trim, and cornice, said to have been carved by "expert Italian workmen." Names of renowned artists are carved into limestone tablets set into blind arches in the brick façade.

At the west side of Abbot Circle is Draper Hall, the central element of the 1886 Hartwell & Richardson master plan. Hartwell & Richardson was a prominent late-nineteenth-century Boston architectural firm, its designs heavily influenced by the work of Henry Hobson Richardson (though William C. Richardson was not related to him). Their master plan for Abbot was similar to one proposed by H. H. Richardson for the Harvard University campus a few years earlier. They designed many public buildings in the Romanesque style, including Christ Church Andover in 1887 and a large commercial block in town in 1890. Draper Hall was one of the firm's largest commissions, and it was this grand scale that made the building a major landmark.

The use of Romanesque detailing and gambrel roofs, while historically incongruous, was part of the intended medieval character of the original design. In a building of this style, with its great massing, no single architectural feature was meant to dominate. The colors of the façade, all having the same tonal value—including the bricks, mortar, shingles, and trim—were designed to blend. The texture of materials also contributed to the overall design and the building's impact. The banks of round-arched windows and ornamented entrance vestibules were typical of Hartwell & Richardson's Romanesque design vocabulary.

The original L-shaped building housed the principal's suite, the library and reading room, two parlors, the academy office, two housekeeping rooms, and sixteen bedrooms and study rooms, on the first floor. Additional bedrooms and eleven music rooms were located on the second and third floors. The fourth floor housed art studios, servants quarters, and

Draper Hall

McKeen Room, Draper Hall

trunk rooms. Most of the service areas were in the basement: kitchen, pantry, dining rooms, laundry and janitor's rooms.

The building stood empty and structurally unsound for 20 years. By 1994 the south wing could not be saved. During demolition, evidence of damage from an 1896 fire that had not been adequately repaired, was uncovered. The main section of the building was restored by Finegold Alexander & Associates, Inc., to its original appearance with a new three-story oriel on the west façade where the wing had been. Copper down-spouts and collection boxes were created from Hartwell & Richardson drawings. All of the shingles were replaced, the brickwork repointed, and brownstone details cleaned. The interior was renovated for faculty housing and administrative offices.

51. McKeen Memorial Hall

Hartwell, Richardson, & Driver, 1903–1904

Named in honor of Philena McKeen, principal of Abbot Academy from 1859 to 1892, this building was central to the academy's attempt to enlarge the campus following the master plan of 1886. It completed Abbot Circle, the heart of the Abbot campus. The sparse ornamentation on the exterior is probably due to the combination of a restricted budget and an attempt by the architects to design a modern building, which would still be compatible with

McKeen Memorial Hall

the out-of-fashion Romanesque style of Draper Hall. The monolithic effect of the brickwork is relieved by a central entrance recessed under a segmented arch and sandstone trim. The copper finials and ridge caps are original.

For years after the merger of Abbot Academy and Phillips Academy, McKeen was used for storage. The interior was renovated in the early 1990s and now houses administrative offices and a community day care center.

52. George E. Abbot Gymnasium *John Radford Abbot, 1955–1956*

By 1952 a new gymnasium was at the top of Abbot Academy's list of building needs. The physical education program was full and existing resources, including Davis Hall, were bursting at the seams. According to Abbot historian Susan Lloyd, pre-war Abbot trustees may have failed to recognize rising interest in women's sports. In any case, serious consideration had never been given to an adequate facility for athletics. By the spring of 1955, Abbot had raised $200,000 for a gym, a scholarship fund, and higher faculty salaries.

John Radford Abbot did a great deal of work remodeling buildings for Abbot and Phillips during the 1940s, 1950s, and 1960s. His design for the Abbot gymnasium is conservative compared to its contemporaries on the Phillips campus [See Walk Five], but he did not have the luxury of an isolated site. He deferred to the three prominent buildings on Abbot Circle. The severe brick block of the gymnasium proper had glass block windows high in the walls, with an adjoining smaller block for offices on the north façade. An entry portico supported by Tuscan columns and surmounted by a wooden parapet provides the only embellishment.

George E. Abbot Gymnasium

After Abbot Academy merged with Phillips in 1973, this gymnasium was no longer needed. The building was renovated for use by the Office of Physical Plant.

53. The Laundry *Hartwell, Richardson, & Driver, 1912*

Abbot Laundry, before restoration

Hartwell, Richardson, & Driver also designed Abbot's laundry building, which was recently saved from demolition by a joint effort of Phillips Academy, SHED, Inc., and the Massachusetts Industrial Finance Agency. O'Neill Pennoyer Architects of Somerville, Massachusetts, restored the old Laundry to its original appearance and erected a new building to accommodate SHED's after-school daycare center.

In the modern world of private schools, outbuildings rarely survive the expansion of a campus. These small buildings were a critical part of student life, for manual labor was considered to be morally beneficial as well as a functional necessity. In a school like Abbot, where architectural design was considered important from the beginning, even the small structures were built with attention to decorative treatments. The laundry building remains an important reminder of the necessities of life in a school before modern conveniences.

Tang Garden   *Child Associates, 1996*
Maple Walk   *Charles W. Gay, 1878*

Maple Walk

The Grove

The Grove, 1890s

In 1878 the trustees hired Charles Gay, a "professional landscape gardener," to develop a master plan for the Abbot campus, about 22 acres. Gay laid out formal drives and paths to connect all the buildings and a semicircular piece of land between Abbot and Smith Halls. At that time, the student entrance to Abbot Hall was on the western or back side, away from the street, and this small half-circle of space was the center of activity. West of Smith Hall, Gay planted an allée of maples, which he intended to go all the way to Phillips Street. He also planned a network of curvilinear roads through the existing oak grove, culminating at a gazebo.

In 1996 after Draper Hall was renovated, the area behind the building was relandscaped by Child Associates of Boston. Individual gardens were created for the first floor faculty apartments. An adjoining sunken terrace with fieldstone walls, named in honor of Frances Young Tang, Abbot Academy 1957, lies immediately to the west. Tang Garden provides a tranquil link to the Maple Walk and the Oak Grove beyond.

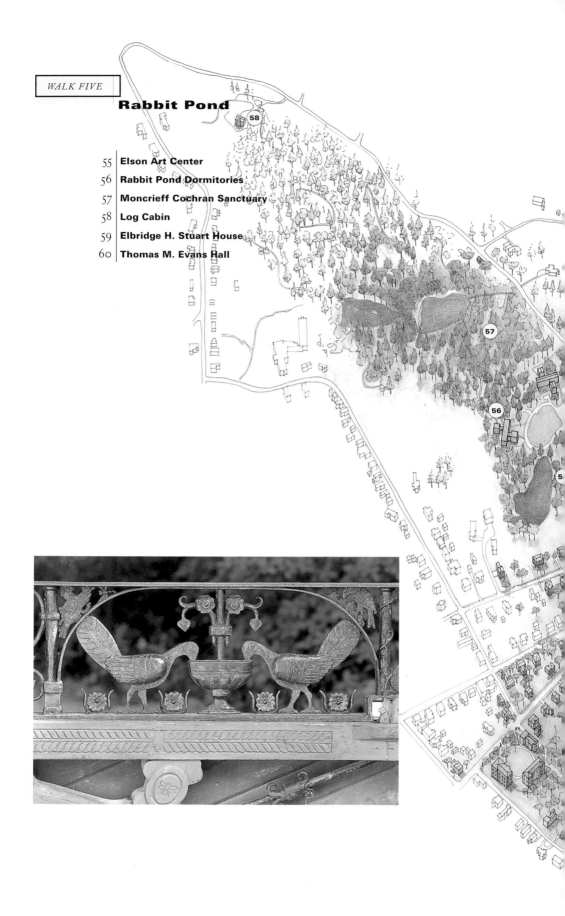

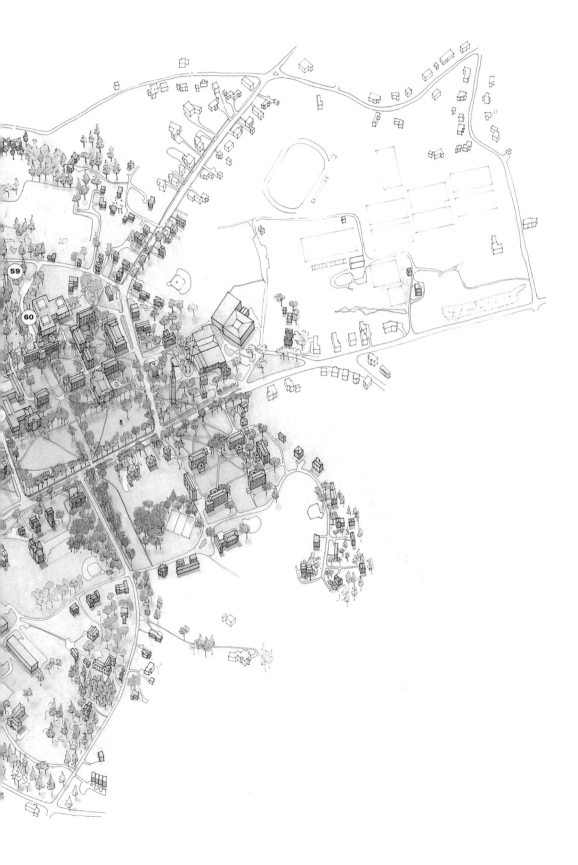

59

60

Modernism Comes to Academy Hill

Rabbit Pond lies at the northeastern corner of the Phillips Academy campus. In addition to the pond itself, which has long been used for recreation by the academy, this area includes the Moncrieff Cochran Sanctuary, and a cluster of five dormitories built in the 1960s. Four of the five were designed by The Architects Collaborative (TAC) of Cambridge. This walk also includes two other TAC projects on campus, the Elson Art Center and Thomas M. Evans Hall.

In the late nineteenth century, Rabbit Pond was a favorite skating spot for students, and for neighborhood children as well. Academy hockey games were played there as early as 1898. The lightly forested area north of the pond was known as Missionary Woods, a reference to the pioneering mission work undertaken by early graduates of the Andover Theological Seminary. In 1910 a granite boulder near Rabbit Pond was dedicated as a

memorial to the students who established the American Society of Missions. The following year the trustees hired the Olmsted firm to prepare plans for a network of roads through Missionary Woods. They intended to subdivide the woods into building lots for sale. In spite of an elaborate plan, no further attempt was made to develop the area.

Missionary Rock

Rabbit Pond

Development of the Moncrieff Cochran Sanctuary, 1929–1930

In 1929 Charles Platt and Thomas Cochran convinced the trustees to set aside that land, and an additional large adjacent tract purchased by Cochran, as a bird sanctuary to be designed by the Olmsted firm. Just as Frederick Law Olmsted and Calvert Vaux had done at New York's Central Park in the mid-nineteenth century, the Olmsteds heavily reworked the existing topography to create a "naturalistic landscape" of ponds, roads, bridges, and indigenous foliage.

The trustees mandated major changes to the area again in the late 1950s and early 1960s when six new dormitories were built near Rabbit Pond on land carved out of the sanctuary. TAC collaborated with a team of faculty, trustees, and administrators of the academy on what was called The Andover Program, projecting future needs for dormitories, art studios, and library space. Founded by the German expatriate architect Walter Gropius, TAC strongly influenced American design after World War II. Gropius believed that modern architecture was particularly appropriate for educational institutions. In 1949 he wrote an article, "Not Gothic but Modern for Our Colleges," for the *New York Times* in which he asked, "How can we expect our students to become bold and fearless in thought and action if we encase them

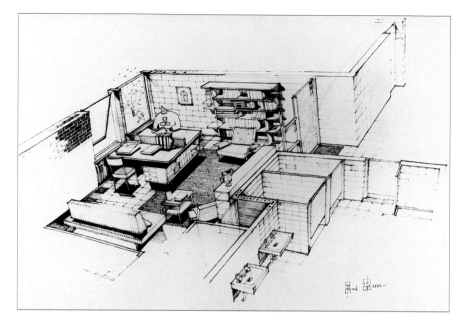

The Architects Collaborative, Dormitory Room

timidly in sentimental shrines feigning a culture which has long since disappeared." Surely, the trustees must have thought that what was good for colleges would also be good for Phillips Academy. One of the highest priorities of The Andover Program was student housing. The academy had grown incrementally since the West Quad was finished in the 1930s and could no longer house all of its boarding students in suitable dormitories. Educational theory was tending away from the old system of master and student toward a more informal relationship. Consequently, architecture began to reflect this new thinking by offering multi-purpose spaces, more relaxed living arrangements, and open classrooms.

The design challenge at Phillips Academy was to fit these radically modern ideas into a campus dominated by historical styles—a revered tradition. At Rabbit Pond, TAC designed four dormitories, nestled in the

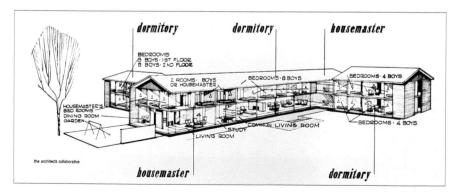

The Architects Collaborative, Schematic Drawing of a Dormitory

naturally hilly terrain of this part of the campus. Benjamin Thompson, former TAC partner, designed a fifth, and a Pietro Belluschi and Jung/Brannen partnership completed the last dorm on a little pine knoll in 1971. The teaching of art and science at the academy had also changed dramatically. Cramped studios in the basement of the Addison Gallery were no longer adequate for the ambitious art curriculum. The science department also required larger quarters where laboratories were flexible in format, and biology, chemistry and physics could all be housed in the same building. Once again, TAC found ingenious ways to satisfy the classroom needs with a fresh new architectural approach.

55. Elson Art Center   *The Architects Collaborative, 1962–1963*

For thirty years, art classes were held in cramped, makeshift spaces in the basement of the Addison Gallery of American Art. By the late fifties it was apparent that the needs of the art program and the needs of the museum could no longer be accommodated in this way. The construction of this building provided the academy with new, light-filled new studios specifically designed to serve the growing art program. Its physical connection with the galleries of the museum was intended to continue the close interaction between the viewing and making of art, and was symbolic of the close relationship between the Addison and the art department. As originally built, the Arts and Communication Center, as it was first called, housed classroom studios for design, painting, photography, pottery, woodworking, sculpture and welding, as well as an audio-visual center and an auditorium. In 1994

Elson Art Center, Courtyard Façade

Elson Art Center, Chapel Avenue

the interior of the building was extensively renovated to meet new air quality standards, to increase studio space and encourage integrated teaching across media, and to add new computer graphic facilities.

The Elson Art Center sits between two Charles Platt buildings, the Addison and George Washington Hall. TAC partner Ben Thompson designed the two-story, L-shaped building as a connector, filling the space between the older buildings with concrete façadess and glass walls. In the wing that connects the art center with the museum, Thompson created a meeting room known as the Underwood Room on the first floor, with full height glass window walls on each side to allow views from the museum courtyard through the building into the art center courtyard. Thompson continued this kind of transparency on the Chapel Avenue side by punching out one of the bays at the first floor to create a low, wide entry that serves as a covered gateway into the new courtyard and beyond into the central campus. The courtyard façades have two floors of large plate glass windows onto studios and hallway galleries, revealing the activity inside to passers-by. Thompson's art center neither overwhelms its older neighbors nor surrenders to their seniority.

56. Rabbit Pond Dormitories

Alfred E. Stearns House   *The Architects Collaborative, 1957*
Abbott Stevens House   *The Architects Collaborative, 1958*
Henry L. Stimson House   *The Architects Collaborative, 1960–1961*
Nathan Hale House   *Benjamin Thompson Associates, 1966*
Claude M. Fuess House   *The Architects Collaborative, 1961–1962*

Stearns House and Stevens House were the first Rabbit Pond dormitories;
they were constructed even before The Andover Program was complete.
With these buildings Ben Thompson, then of TAC, established the vocabulary that he would use on three more houses over the next nine years. First,
Thompson elected to use red brick as his primary material, as a gesture to
builders who came before him. Then he expanded the use of glass to wall-
size sheets, far larger than anything used on campus previously. He set the
brick and glass walls on concrete platforms recessed under concrete piers
and wide concrete roof overhangs. The siting of these buildings is just as
radical as their architecture. Each of the Rabbit Pond dorms is nestled into
the surrounding landscape, apparently set down amongst existing trees and
disrupting the natural topography as little as possible. The architect chose
to mediate the impact of the modern style of the dormitories through a
combination of sympathetic materials, irregular plans, gable roofs, and
informal siting. This style is in dramatic contrast to the rest of the campus,
where buildings were set in prominent sites and in close relation to each
other in order to enclose or suggest distinct landscape areas.

     The trustees and faculty were well aware that they were departing
from the ordinary. Simeon Hyde, chairman of the faculty committee on

Abbott Stevens House

Nathan Hale House

the new dormitories, wrote, "With less effort and expense we might have duplicated the familiar brick dormitory; instead we have poured into the ground the outline of a new way of living. We have ventured in the hope of gain. . . . The new dormitories are tangible evidence of the continuing force of an Andover tradition—the creative approach to the problems of the day."

Stimson House, Hale House, and Fuess House are variations on the theme established at Stearns and Stevens. They vary in configuration, according to their sites, but not in their intent to coexist with their natural surroundings and provide the best possible built environment for young adults. Like Stearns and Stevens, each dorm was designed for forty students, in units of eight boys each, and two housemasters and their families. Privacy and independence were priorities but a large common living area bridged the gap between boys and adults. According to The Andover Program, this room was the "heart of the new dormitory concept . . . an extension of the senior housemaster's study. The aim is to provide a natural meeting ground for housemaster and his boys."

Thompson designed Hale House for the academy, after he had left TAC to establish his own firm, Benjamin Thompson Associates. He sited the dormitory, the only one of the group designed with an international style flat roof, on slightly higher wooded ground than the others, between the sanctuary and Rabbit Pond. In its brick courtyard in a bronze statue of the patriot Nathan Hale by sculptor Bela Pratt.

57. Moncrieff Cochran Sanctuary

Olmsted Brothers, 1929–1930

Gates close at dusk.

Sanctuary gates

Between Hale House and Fuess House is the entrance to the sanctuary, a charming stone and wood gate designed by the artist Stuart Travis. Travis worked on the Andover campus for many years, painting murals in the Oliver Wendell Holmes Library and the Peabody Museum. For the sanctuary gate, he chose rusticated lumber construction, supported by stone piers, and topped with an appealing frieze of birds and flowers in wrought iron. These gates were originally built in 1932 near the old cemetery on an access road to the sanctuary. When the school appropriated the northwest portion of the sanctuary for the Rabbit Pond dormitories, the gates were moved to their present location.

The bird sanctuary began modestly enough, with the construction of two small islands in Rabbit Pond for duck shelters. Platt and Cochran, never satisfied with less than spectacular results, soon were concocting a bigger and better version. With the Olmsteds' expertise and a virtually unlimited budget provided by Cochran, they completely changed the face of the old Missionary Woods and adjoining fields. Between the spring of 1929 and the spring of 1930 they dammed an existing stream to create two new ponds, laid out three miles of gravel roads and built bridges for pedestrian traffic. They added dozens of new azalea, wild blueberry, laurel, and rhododendron bushes to the naturally wooded site. Finally, hundreds of birds—ducks, geese, swans, quail, and pheasants—were brought in, all for the edification and enjoyment of the academy boys. To protect the birds from predators, they fenced the whole site, reportedly at a cost of $39,000.

This ambitious sanctuary proved to be very expensive to maintain. After Cochran's death, the trustees decided to surrender the concept of a refuge, and the birds were sold or released to the wild. Over the years, the plantings have been allowed to naturalize. The dam, however, is carefully monitored as a flood control precaution. Today, the sanctuary is used year-round as a quiet retreat from the hustle and bustle of everyday life.

Moncrieff Cochran Sanctuary

58. Log Cabin *1929*

At the eastern end of the sanctuary, a large, one-room log cabin with a stone fireplace was constructed as a gathering place for students. The use of a log cabin style for recreation-related buildings, such as summer cottages, was very popular in the 1920s and 1930s. The design of this cabin is typical of others built at the time. After the sanctuary was completed, generous alumni donated sleeping bags and camping gear to the Log Cabin, so that the boys could enjoy fully the woodsy retreat.

Log cabin

59. Elbridge H. Stuart House

Pietro Belluschi & Jung/Brannen, Associate Architects, 1970

The first major dormitory constructed after The Andover Programn, Elbridge Stuart House is compatible with scale and configuration of the TAC-designed structures closer to the pond. This building is well suited to its site, a heavily forested pine knoll. In this case, the architects chose vertical wood siding, wood window trim, and wide overhanging eaves, rather than the brick, concrete, and glass of the TAC dorms.

Elbridge H. Stuart House

60. Thomas M. Evans Hall

The Architects Collaborative, 1961–1963

Ben Thompson's success with the early Rabbit Pond dorms led to additional commissions on campus. Thomas M. Evans Hall was the product of the "flexible laboratory" concept of 1960s science education. Biology, chemistry and physics each occupied a wing, with movable partitions.

Evans was designed to stand alone behind Samuel Phillips Hall, and has been described as a modern outdoor sculpture, independent of other campus buildings. As architectural historian Paul V. Turner has observed of both Evans Hall and the Elson Art Center, these buildings

> embodied new planning concepts that emerged in the postwar years. In contrast to classical principles of proportion and proper distances between buildings, the new 'rules' allowed asymmetry, existing buildings to be connected with new construction, and buildings even placed in the middle of spaces rather than at their edges.

Other projects had been proposed for this location before. Guy Lowell had designed a classroom building for this site, that would have closed off the southeast corner of the Great Quad. [See Walk One] This was also one of the alternate sites for Charles Platt's infirmary of 1929. In 1945 the school commissioned Perry, Shaw, & Hepburn to design a student union here as a memorial to Phillips Academy alumni killed in World War II; the Olmsted firm designed an elaborate landscaping plan for the site. None of these proposals ever went further than the drawing board. Because a

Thomas M. Evans Hall

Rabbit Pond

school's campus is not a static, immutable monument, and must grow and change to accommodate new academic and space initiatives, the trustees commissioned a master plan for the entire Phillips Academy campus in 1994. Among other important conclusions and directions, that study identified the area around Evans Hall toward Highland Road as a potential location of future growth of the school and its campus.

Bibliography

Repositories

Phillips Academy Archive

Phillips Academy Office of Physical Plant

Andover [Massachusetts] Historical Society

Andover Newton Theological Seminary Archive

Avery Library, Columbia University

Boston Public Library

Frederick Law Olmsted National Historic Site, National Park Service

Manuscript Division, Library of Congress

MIT Museum Architecture & Design Collection

MIT Museum Historical Collections

Journals, Newspapers and Unpublished Work

The Phillips Bulletin

The Mirror

The Phillipian

The Andover Townsman

The Andover Advertiser

The Lawrence American

The Andover Program. Andover, Mass.: Phillips Academy, 1958.

Downs, Annie Sawyer. *Abbot Academy, Andover, and its New Buildings.* Boston: The New England Magazine, 1886. [Reprinted from *The New England Magazine*, February, 1886.]

Prentice & Chan, Ohlhausen. *The Campus Master Plan.* unpublished, 1996.

Reed, Roger. *Phillips Academy Historical Buildings and Landscapes Survey.* unpublished, 1994.

Publications

Addison Gallery of American Art. *Academy Hill: The Andover Campus, 1778 to the Present.* Andover, MA, and New York: Addison Gallery of American Art and Princeton Architectural Press, 2000.

Abbot, Abiel. *History of Andover from its settlement to 1829.* Andover, MA: Flagg and Gould, 1829.

Allis, Frederick S., Jr. *Youth From Every Quarter: A Bicentennial History of Phillips Academy, Andover.* Andover, MA: Phillips Academy, 1979.

Bailey, Sarah L. *Historical Sketches of Andover.* Boston: Houghton, Mifflin, 1880.

Carpenter, C. C. *Biographical Catalogue of the Trustees, Teachers & Students of Phillips Academy, Andover, 1778–1830.* Andover, MA: Phillips Academy, 1903.

Carpenter, Jane B. *Abbot & Miss Bailey & Abbot in the Early Years.* Andover, MA: Abbot Academy, 1959.

Chamberlain, Ernest B. *Our Independent Schools.* New York: American Book Co., 1944.

Domingue, Robert A. *Phillips Academy, Andover, Massachusetts: An Illustrated History of the Property (Including Abbot Academy).* Wilmington, MA: The Hampshire Press, 1990.

Fagan, Charles A., IV. "Charles Bulfinch, Peter Banner, and Andover Hill." *Essex Institute Historical Collections* 75 (April 1989): 177–95.

Fuess, Claude Moore. *An Old New England School, A History of Phillips Academy, Andover.* Boston: Houghton Mifflin Company, 1917.

Fuess, Claude Moore. *Independent Schoolmaster*. Boston: Little, Brown and Company, 1952.

Gary, Loren, ed. *A Widening Circle: Abbot Academy and the Abiding Significance of Place.* Andover, MA: Phillips Academy, 1997.

Greven, Philip J. Jr. *Four Generations: Population, Land, and Family in Colonial Andover, Massachusetts.* Ithaca and London: Cornell University Press, 1970.

Harrison, Fred. *Athletics for All: Physical Education and Athletics at Phillips Academy.* Andover, MA: Phillips Academy, 1983.

Horowitz, Helen Lefkowitz. *Alma Mater: Design and Experience in the Women's Colleges from Their Nineteenth-Century Beginnings to the 1930s.* New York: Alfred A. Knopf, 1984.

Kelsey, Katherine R. *Abbot Academy Sketches 1892–1912.* Boston: Houghton Mifflin Company, 1929.

Kemper, John Mason. *Phillips Academy at Andover, A National Public School.* New York: Newcomen Society of North America, 1957.

Lloyd, Susan McIntosh. *A Singular School: Abbot Academy 1828–1973.* Andover, MA: Phillips Academy, 1979.

Marr, Harriet Webster. *The Old New England Academies.* New York: Comet Press Book, 1959.

McKeen, Philena and Phebe F. *Annals of Fifty Years: A History of Abbot Academy, Andover, Mass., 1829–1879.* Andover, MA: Warren F. Draper, 1880.

McKeen, Philena. *Sequel to Annals of Fifty Years: A History of Abbot Academy, Andover, Mass., 1879–1892.* Andover, MA: Warren F. Draper, 1897.

McLachlan, James. *American Boarding Schools: A Historical Study.* New York: Scribner, 1970.

Morgan, Keith N. *Charles A. Platt: The Artist as Architect.* New York and Cambridge: The Architectural History Foundation and The MIT Press, 1985.

Park, William E. *The Earlier Annals of Phillips Academy.* Andover, MA: Phillips Academy, 1878.

Robbins, Sarah Stuart. *Old Andover Days: Memories of a Puritan Childhood.* Boston: The Pilgrim Press, 1908.

Rowe, Henry K. *History of Andover Theological Seminary.* Newton, MA: Thomas Todd Company, Printers, 1933.

Sizer, Theodore R., ed. *The Age of the Academies.* New York: Teachers College, Columbia University, 1964.

Taylor, John L. *A Memoir of His Honor Samuel Phillips, LLD.* Boston: Congregational Board of Publication, 1856.

Turner, Paul V. *Campus: An American Planning Tradition.* Cambridge, Mass.: The MIT Press, 1984.

Woods, Leonard. *History of the Andover Theological Seminary.* Boston: James R. Osgood, 1885.

Zaitzevsky, Cynthia. *Frederick Law Olmsted and the Boston Park System.* Cambridge, MA: Belknap Press, 1982.

Illustration credits

All color photographs are copyright © 2000 Walter Smalling Jr., unless noted below. All black and white photographs of historic images from the Phillips Academy Archive and by Frank W. Graham, unless noted below.

pp. vi, "Circling Round," 99, 109 bottom: Photograph by Greg Heins

p. 29: Courtesy of David P. Handlin & Associates, Cambridge, Massachusetts

p. 37: copyright © Richard Cheek

pp. 48, 81, 89, 108 top, 116, 121 bottom, 122: Raymond Sprague, courtesy of Phillips Academy Office of Physical Plant

pp. 49, 83: Photograph by Michael E. Williams, courtesy of Phillips Academy Office of Physical Plant

pp. 74, 75, 113: National Park Service, Frederick Law Olmsted National Historic Site, Brookline, Massachusetts

Cherubic capital in Cochran Chapel

Index

(*Italics* indicates a photograph.)